The Aims of Education

The Aims of Education
(Glaucon)

M V C Jeffreys

Pitman Publishing

First published as "Glaucon" 1950
Revised and reprinted 1955
Reprinted 1957, 1960, 1961, 1963, 1964
First published in this edition 1972

Sir Isaac Pitman and Sons Ltd
Pitman House, Parker Street, Kingsway, London WC2B 5PB
PO Box 46038, Portal Street, Nairobi, Kenya

Sir Isaac Pitman (Aust) Pty Ltd
Pitman House, Bouverie Street, Carlton, Victoria 3053, Australia

Pitman Publishing Company SA Ltd
PO Box 11231, Johannesburg, South Africa

Pitman Publishing Corporation
6 East 43rd Street, New York, NY 10017, USA

Sir Isaac Pitman (Canada) Ltd
495 Wellington Street West, Toronto 135, Canada

The Copp Clark Publishing Company
517 Wellington Street West, Toronto 135, Canada

© M V C Jeffreys 1972

Cased edition ISBN: 0 273 36085 X
Paperback edition ISBN: 0 273 36163 5

Printed by photo-lithography and made in Great Britain at
the Pitman Press, Bath
G2—(G.4648/4664:15)

Preface

THE plan of this book needs a word of explanation, since it has a unity which might not be immediately apparent from the Table of Contents. To a large extent the field of inquiry is the same in Parts I and II, but the standpoint is different. While Part II assumes Christian belief, Part I does not. Part I is an attempt to examine empirically the nature and purpose of education in relation to history and society; this inquiry leads to certain unanswered questions, and, in fact, leaves the whole issue incomplete. Part II attempts to show how far a Christian philosophy fulfils the implicit intimations of the empirical inquiry; that is to say, Part II gives the antiphonal response to Part I. The keynote of Part I is the value of human personality, and the nurture of personal growth is found to be the essential meaning of education. The question why human personality is of supreme value cannot be answered in Part I, nor can there be any resolution of the paradox of man as a creature at odds with himself, who has to lose himself to find himself. It is when these universal human problems are re-examined in the light of Christian belief about man and God that they are seen to make sense. The keynote of Part II is Christ Crucified, Who is both the darkest mystery of human existence and the one true Light.

The book attempts in some sense to do what has not been done before. It is therefore experimental. Inevitably it is also sketchy, because the ground covered is very extensive. That it has many errors and weaknesses I have no doubt, and I am painfully aware that I do not always manage to say what I mean. I would ask that the book should be judged as a piece of reconnaissance in a field where a great deal of important work is waiting to be done.

My acknowledgments are due to the proprietors of the *Schoolmaster* for permission to use some material included in Chapter VI, and to The Adult School Union for permission to use some passages from a lecture delivered at Nottingham in October, 1948.   M. V. C. JEFFREYS

Note To The Second Impression

I HAVE revised the text in a good many places, in the light of criticism for which I am grateful. In particular I wish to acknowledge the valuable advice and help given me by Professor L. A. Reid, after consultation with whom I have re-written the passage on determinism and free will in Chapter III.

                                         M. V. C. JEFFREYS

Contents

viii

Introduction to this Edition

A GOOD deal has happened in the world since the original publication of this book twenty years ago. Technology has advanced prodigiously, mainly through the development of electronics and synthetic materials. Space travel and computers no longer surprise us.

But technical progress has not, on balance, eased the problems of modern civilization. We live in a time of mounting economic and political tensions. Inflation, attended by the rising cost of living and labour troubles, defeats one government after another.

Although we have so far had no third World War, and open conflict between world powers has been kept within the limits of indirect and peripheral encounter, there has been so notable an increase of domestic disturbance in the Western countries as to suggest that there may be forces at work trying to disrupt Western civilization from within. While the democracies have been proving how vulnerable they are, events in Hungary and Czechoslovakia have shown what happens to liberalizing efforts under the Eastern authoritarian régimes.

Culturally, the last twenty years in the West have seen a landslide of established traditions and values, without much sign as yet of their replacement by anything constructive. A new phenomenon is the anarchist mentality, which recognizes no obligation to offer a positive alternative to what is to be destroyed. The "permissive society," illustrated on stage and film, and in literature, is scarcely the solution of any human problem. No doubt there are sincere experimenters who seek some kind of truth. We may hope they find it. Meanwhile, it has to be recognized that permissiveness is not freedom, but the erosion of discrimination, and so of meaning, and is therefore a prescription for ultimate and unlimited boredom.

The world of education naturally reflects the characteristics of the larger world. In education, as in our whole civilization, we see great progress in techniques combined with doubt and confusion about aims. On the one hand is all the experimental work with programmed learning, teaching machines, and the rest. These developments may prove to be great blessings, both by improving the learning process and by releasing teachers for more human activities; though we should note the risk that accompanies all technical progress—the danger lest we be seduced into doing, and regarding as most important, those things which the machines can do, and so of becoming slaves instead of masters of the machines. The *Bulletin* of the University of London Institute of Education for Autumn, 1970, contains an interesting article by Norman E. Willis on the work of the National Council for Educational Technology, a body established in 1967 on the recommendation of the Brynmor Jones Report (1965) on Audio-Visual Aids in Higher Scientific Education.

Notwithstanding the rapid progress in educational techniques, the secondary curriculum has been described as a "non-curriculum," and in the last ten years there has been considerable concern, both in schools and universities, about the content of secondary education. The question is not only what should be learned, but what should be the active relation between the various "subjects," and between the curriculum and the concerns of real life. Since the Crowther Report of 1959, there have been six proposals for curriculum reform. If nothing very much has happened, we must remember that education is necessarily a conservative business, because teachers are equipped to teach what was taught when they were trained, and (in secondary schools at any rate) few of them have time to re-equip themselves as well as doing their day-to-day work.

The *Schools Council Report for 1969–70* shows that, in that period, some 70 research projects in aspects of the curriculum were going on, promoted either by the Schools Council alone or by the Council together with another body, such as the Nuffield Foundation. In most cases the actual research has been centred at a university or college. A few of the most relevant projects, in the present context, are: Social Studies (8–13), the whole curriculum for the Middle Years of Schooling (8–13), Social Education (11–16), Integration of the Humanities (11–16), and General Studies (15–18). Readers who are interested in the work that is being done on the curriculum can apply to the Schools Council, 160, Great Portland Street, London, W.1, for their list of publications, and could profitably study the *Bulletin* of the University of London Institute of Education for Autumn, 1969, and Spring, 1970.

One of the most controversial problems of curriculum is that of Religious Education. In this field there is much contemporary controversy about the aims, methods and content of religious education in schools. The secularists have become more vocal of late, and some demand that the requirement of R.E. should be dropped from a new Education Act. The prevailing opinion, however, still is that R.E. should be available to all pupils unless they or their parents opt against it. The main cleavage of opinion is on the issue of "indoctrination"—an unfortunate word that generates more heat than light. On the one side are those who, while recognizing the right and responsibility of the individual to think his own way to the truth, believe that the Christian teacher and the Christian school should present positively what they believe the Christian faith to be. People of this way of thinking see no necessary conflict between positive teaching and the active cultivation of the pupil's capacity to think for himself. And they point out that religion, to be properly understood, must be experienced and not merely observed. On the other side are those who maintain that the business of R.E. is not to "teach religion," but rather to teach *about* religion. They tell us that religious education should be "open-ended," and they remind us that Christianity is only one of the religions to be found in this country now.*

The curriculum, and its relevance to life, is not the only educational problem whose temperature has risen. The organization of education, especially at the secondary level, has become a

---

* This whole controversy is discussed in my *Truth is not Neutral*, R.E.P., 1969.

xii

matter of fierce controversy, and has been dragged into the political arena. The last Labour Government, especially since the General Election of 1966, made every effort to get the Local Education Authorities to adopt thorough-going Comprehensive programmes. The Conservative Government, elected in the summer of 1970, has relieved the L.E.A.'s from the pressure to "go Comprehensive."* The great difficulty, in debates about the organization of the educational system, is to keep clear the distinctions between party-political and genuinely educational objectives (which are easily confused in such a phrase as "equality of opportunity"), and between substance and shadow (a Comprehensive school is not created by a decree that, as from tomorrow, Grammar School A and Modern Schools B, C, and D shall be deemed to constitute the Q Comprehensive School).

Meanwhile, the universities are in turmoil. Twenty years ago we were not greatly worried about teenage drug-addiction, and we had scarcely heard of "student power." Today there is hardly a Vice-Chancellor who has not been ousted from his office-premises by a sit-in, or scandalized by rude graphiti or nudity on the campus. In November, 1970, the University of Reading cancelled a dinner in honour of their new Chancellor, Lord Sherfield, because some students objected to his former business connections with South Africa; and the University of East Anglia transferred part of its account from a bank which was financially involved with South Africa, in order to ease the consciences of students who would not pay their fees. In the same month a letter to the Press suggested that students who want to be consistent in their opposition to apartheid might consider renouncing their grants, received from the British Government which has long-established commercial connections with South Africa.†

* The issues involved, both educational and political, are discussed in my *The Unity of Education*, R.E.P., 1966.
† One of the most disturbing accounts of a new university yet published was R. Barry O'Brien's article on the University of Essex in the *Daily Telegraph*, November 26, 1970. In the Reith Lectures for 1963, the Vice-Chancellor, Dr. Alfred Sloman, said that the aim of the new university was to give students "an adult environment" with a minimum of rules. Mr. O'Brien's account suggests that, seven years later, the scheme is not working very well, and that students are listless and unhappy. The university authorities, he suggests, would

The tribulations of the universities have had plenty of publicity. What is perhaps more worthy of comment here is the new concern of the universities about their social relevance. They are aware, as perhaps never before, of the need not only to justify their degree courses as equipping people for special functions in society but also to provide direct services and amenities for the community around them. An important recent piece of work is the survey, by Dr. Joyce Long, *Universities and the General Public* (University of Birmingham Educational Review Occasional Publications, No. 3, 1968). Through music and drama, and in other ways, the universities today are contributing to the life of the local community far more than they did twenty years ago.* The strictures on Arts Faculties in the first edition of this book (pp. 98–9) are far less deserved today than they were then.

. . . .

The double theme of this book is that, from the point of view of the individual, education is the nurture of personal growth; and, from the point of view of the community, the function of education is to conserve, transmit and renew culture. Individual and community are inextricably involved with one another because neither can exist without the other, and because, to a large extent, the quality of a community is determined by that of the individuals who compose it, and the quality of individuals is influenced by that of the community in which they live. In the last resort, however, we must attribute ultimate value to the individual. There is a sense in which, as Aristotle said, the State is prior to the individual. But there is a deeper sense in which ultimate value belongs to the individual. Apart from the actual human beings who constitute it, a community is an empty abstraction. Individual human beings, however much they may be influenced by others and by circumstances, are the efficient source of social change. Societies as such cannot think; they

---

find it difficult to back out of a policy to which they are committed, and so go on hoping for the best. It is only fair to record that Mr. O'Brien's criticisms have themselves been criticized by members of the university's teaching staff.

* See also my *The Unity of Education* (Ch. 4), R.E.P., 1966, and *The Ministry of Teaching* (Ch. 4), Pitman, 1967.

cannot imagine, discover, create; these are the functions of individuals. As Sir Percy Nunn wrote half a century ago: "Nothing good enters into the human world except in and through the free activities of individual men and women."

The main emphasis of this book, then, is on what, in a kind of shorthand, may be called personal values. The most important business of education is to help young people to grow as rational and responsible persons, in fellowship with others. This task has become more, not less, urgent during the past twenty years. The threat to personal values is greater now than it was then. The outlines of the picture are clearer. The hazards of the technological civilization are more obvious. Although, in economic terms, today's citizen has more opportunity for choice than ever before, his choice is increasingly unreal. More and more we have our thinking done for us and our lives ordered for us. Man, in fact, takes on the image of the machine.

To say this is by no means to condemn modern technology, which can be an unlimited power for good if rightly used. The technological civilization, like any other, is as good or bad as the people who operate it. Technology is an *instrument*; it has no magic in itself to make the world better. The most important thing in the life of society, and the deepest concern of education, is the quality of people.

It stands to reason that, if education is supremely concerned with the quality of people, it needs the inspiration of some vision of what human beings ought to be—some notion of what is a good kind of person, or a bad kind of person. This is a moral and spiritual question, and one to which it is very difficult to get a clear and united answer in these days of confused and disintegrating values. The trouble about our present condition is that we know more and more about means, and less and less about ends. Our traditional architecture of values, both moral and aesthetic, is dilapidated. The very foundations of our civilization seem to be threatened; and—possibly for the first time since the decay of the Roman Empire—people today can talk soberly about the possibility of a collapse of western civilization as we know it. There would seem to be three ways in which our civilization might come to an end. It might blow itself up. It might poison itself. And it might die on its feet—because it ceased to mean anything. These three fates—explosion, pollution, and boredom—might provide material for a sardonic party game. It is not, however, in the nature of man to despair. Nothing is inevitable until it has happened. We must, however, be realistic. Whether we look to the East or to the West, we have cause for uneasiness. In the East we see Collectivism, with its optimistic belief that the efficient organization of society will eventually bring satisfaction to all. In the West we see Individualism, with its optimistic belief that, if everyone has a chance in the rat-race, everyone in the end will benefit.

If our western tradition of liberal democracy is to survive, we must be prepared to make the effort necessary for its survival. There is no magic in democracy which makes it self-supporting and self-perpetuating. On the contrary, it is the most difficult form of government to maintain. We need, in time of peace, the heroic qualities (idealism, courage, self-discipline) that are called forth in time of war. We can perhaps learn something from the Communist powers, which have the wisdom to keep the tempo of life keyed up for perpetual struggle. The kind of world that we want for ourselves and our children will not come by sitting back to enjoy the amenities of the affluent society, and getting as much as we can for doing as little as possible.

Ours is a difficult world for young people. The outlook, however, is by no means all dark. It is dangerous to generalize about moral standards. There may have been a decline in the standards of private morality; but the social conscience of this generation is possibly more active than ever before, partly because improved communications bring us knowledge of what is going on in other parts of the world, and partly because the different parts of the world are more materially interdependent than ever before. Youthful idealism is not always balanced or well thought out. But there is plenty of evidence—in such enterprises as Voluntary Service Overseas—of a great capacity among young people for adventure and unselfish service.

Nor should we forget the great extent to which the social

conscience has been channelled into public service. It is easy to find fault with the Welfare State, which certainly has its defects and its dangers. But, almost entirely within the last fifty years, a system of social services has been created which would have amazed our grandparents. It is salutary to study the *Consumer's Guide to the British Social Services**—a remarkably clear, complete and concise description of what the Welfare State means in terms of the practical problems of ordinary people's lives. Supporting the public services, and co-operating with them, there are in this country about a thousand voluntary societies and institutions, whose activities represent an enormous potential of good will.†

The great virtue of voluntary service is that it *is* voluntary. It works like leaven to regenerate society by affirming the basic human values of respect for honest work and the respect of one human being for another. It affirms a viable alternative to cut-throat competition on one side and totalitarian control on the other.

Lord Beveridge wrote his notable book, *Voluntary Action*, under the shadow of post-war disillusionment.‡ He writes sadly of the passing of the robust idealism that inspired the Victorian pioneers of social progress—Shaftesbury, Elizabeth Fry, the Barnetts, the Booths. "None of the Victorian pioneers dreamed of a world with dangers such as ours. None of them doubted that man could and would be master of his fate." Yet he could believe in a new dawn, when "the night's insane dream of power over other men, without limit and without mercy, shall fade. So mankind in brotherhood shall bring back the day."§ It would be interesting to know what Lord Beveridge, who saw things so clearly, and did so much to help in building the Welfare State, would have thought of the world of 1971. At all events, while there is life there is hope.

* By Phyllis Willmott, Penguin Books, 1967.
† See Ch. 7 of my *Personal Values in the Modern World*, Penguin Books.
‡ Published 1948.
§ *Voluntary Action*, p. 323.

Part I

Education and Modern Society

"The central value—or, to put it another way, the value
that includes all our other values—is respect for personality."
                    Victor Gollancz: *Our Threatened Values, p. 9*

I
The Nature of Education

IT IS good for teachers to remember that parents brought up their children in the life of the tribe long before schools and schoolmasters were thought of, and for professors of education to acknowledge that they are a recent excrescence on the educational structure. Education is in fact nothing other than the whole life of a community viewed from the particular standpoint of learning to live that life.

Education therefore cannot be conducted *in vacuo*. What we believe about education implicates our beliefs about everything else. The ends and means of education must be seen in relation to the ultimate problems of life—problems that concern the nature and destiny of man both as a member of historically developing society and as a being in the presence of eternity. Whereas, from one point of view education is a specialized study, with its own techniques, and is the business of experts, from another point of view education is everyone's business and involves everything that living itself involves. The process of intellectual, emotional, and social growth is susceptible of expert investigation, and affords a valid group of appropriate disciplines. At the same time, none of us can escape active participation in the business of education, our own and other people's, since the influence of persons upon one another must result in education of some kind, good, bad, or indifferent.

Personal Growth

It would be generally agreed that the aim of education is the full and balanced development of persons. The emphasis that has been laid in recent years upon "the education of the whole child" reflects not so much a new discovery about education as our uneasiness lest education should be failing in its acknowledged purpose under the increasingly difficult conditions of modern life. What that purpose is can perhaps be conveniently crystallized in the formula: *Nurture of Personal Growth*. The terms of this formula have been carefully chosen and need some exposition.

First, *Growth*. The development of a living thing differs from a process of manufacture in this important respect: the meaning and value of a living thing belongs to it at all stages of its growth whereas a process of manufacture is meaningless apart from the end-product. Putting that differently, manufacture is a means to an end, while growth is an end in itself. If a man has a right to live, so has a child. If human life is sacred, it does not begin to be sacred at the age of twenty-one, but is sacred at all ages. In the factory, the whole conveyor-belt process is wasted unless the motor-car comes out complete at the end. In the family, if a member dies young, his short life and limited achievements have their own unique and irreplaceable value. Not only that; the law of growth demands the fulfilment of each stage of development for its own sake, as it comes, and not only as a preparation for some hypothetical end-product. There is, in fact, no end-product in the sense of a stage at which it is possible to say: The process is now complete; nothing remains to be done. This is a first principle in education, and the duty of the educator is to enable the growing person to make the best of himself at the stage he has reached. The best preparation for the future is to respond fully to the challenge of the present. In the words of Sir John Adams: "Childhood has a meaning and a value in itself apart from its value as a step on the way to maturity. The better the child; that is, the truer he is to his child nature as such, the better man will he make when the proper time comes."*

In education we are dealing not only with growth, as distinct from manufacture, but with growth at a particular level. The word *personal* is used to indicate the rational and moral level as contrasted with the instinctive level of the animals. It is true that man is animal and carries with him the whole of his animal heritage. But it is also true (and this is the source of man's spiritual discomfort) that man transcends the animal so that his nature will never allow him to make a success of life at the animal

* *The Evolution of Educational Theory*, p. 63.

level. No mere adjustment of stimulus and response at the level of appetite can bring man happiness. His problems of adjustment are never problems of *external* adjustment only. The restlessness and homelessness of the human spirit have their origin ultimately within man himself. Therefore there can be no "natural" solution of man's problems. As it has been neatly put, man's nature is ever to be dissatisfied with "nature." If he yields to the temptation to subside on to the "natural" level, he "makes a beast of himself"; and the beastliness of man is something quite different from the naturalness of the beast. Animal though he is, man is nevertheless compelled from within himself to repudiate the animal and to strive for a synthesis of his powers at the rational and moral level. In this attempt man is on the whole remarkably unsuccessful, and history is in the main the record of his failure. More than that: were it not for man's internal conflict, making him a creature at odds with himself, man would have no history. The creatures of instinct, whose problems of adjustment are external only, may have civilization, as do bees and ants, but they have no history. History is man's struggle with himself. Man's first step towards coping realistically with his problems is to recognize his contradictory nature and the resulting conflict concentrated within the microcosm of the individual self and amplified in the macrocosm of history. He must recognize that human destiny is cast in the dimensions of heaven and hell rather than of plain earth, and that it is the tension between heaven and hell, not the tranquillity of earth, that gives human life its distinctive character. He must, in fact, have a sense of sin, which is an entirely different thing from morbid guilt; the one is the acceptance and the other is the rejection of the plain meaning of experience.

The third term in the formula is *nurture*. Personal growth thrives neither under compulsion nor under neglect. The educator's function, like the gardener's, is to provide the best possible conditions for right development—that is, to create opportunity. Growth is something that the organism itself does. No one can grow for another, nor learn for another. Yet continual help is needed if growth is to be full. And the higher in the scale of life, the greater is the need for help in growing, and (to say the same thing in another way) the longer and more significant is the period of childhood. Insects, once the egg is laid, are independent of their parents. Kittens and puppies need their parents obviously and for some time, but the need, as far as we can judge, is mainly if not entirely physical. Of all the animals man has the longest childhood, the most helpless infancy, and the widest range of needs. His growth depends on mental and spiritual as well as bodily help. And the educator must know not only what to do but what not to do; that is to say, he must respect freedom and know when to stand back, recognizing that freedom necessarily includes liberty to make mistakes. The late Dr. H. G. Stead was fond of quoting, as epitomizing the whole duty of the teacher, two sayings from the Fourth Gospel: "I came that they might have life" and "It is expedient for you that I go away."*

Conservation, Transmission, and Renewal of Culture

Although education is properly thought of in terms of personal growth, it is equally valid to look at education as a social instrument. Education, that is to say, is the community's means of doing something with its heritage of knowledge, ideas, and attitudes. Whereas a system of education can obviously be a passive reflection of an existing social order, it can also be an instrument for changing that social order. History can furnish examples of educational systems which have been deliberately planned and effectively used in order to produce certain social results. It is enough to think of the education of the Spartan, the medieval knight, the Nazi, and the Soviet citizen in order to be reminded of the power of education to produce not only a kind of person but a kind of society. We can also reflect on the importance of the new techniques for collectively influencing opinion (wireless and the cinema) in strengthening the social power of education. And we can speculate on the factors that determine the extent to which education is a passive reflection of a social order or an active agent of social change. Broadly

* John x. 10 and xvi. 7.

speaking the answer to this last question would appear to be that in a tranquil society the educational system will tend to reflect the social pattern, while social uneasiness and instability create opportunity for using education as an instrument of social change.

In order to define the social function of education it is convenient to make use of two other words, civilization and culture. In the present context "civilization" is used for social structure and function, whereas "culture" denotes our interpretation of that structure and function. Culture, in fact, is what we think of our civilization. Animals as well as man have civilization. But, so far as we know, man alone has culture. We have no evidence that animals think about their social organization, form beliefs, or keep records.

It is clear that, in a healthy society, culture ought to interpret the civilization that exists and not one that has ceased to exist or never existed. Now education is manifestly a cultural instrument, and its function is the three-fold one of conserving, transmitting, and renewing culture. Education is therefore very much concerned with the proper relation between culture and civilization. If culture is to be in living relation to civilization, sensitively responding to social change and anticipating social adjustment, education must pay as much attention to the work of renewal as to that of conservation. The three things, civilization, culture, and education, are in fact connected in such a way that none of the three can be healthy unless all three are in proper relation to one another. If the culture of a community is out of gear with its civilization—if, for example, the culture represents a social pattern and social values which no longer exist—the education of that community, using the obsolete culture as its material, is bound to be ineffective and unreal. By the same token, when seeking the causes of defects in a system of education, it is wise to examine the relation between the culture and civilization of the society in question. On the other hand, given a live and healthy relation between civilization and culture, the educational system of such a society is unlikely to have much wrong with it that cannot fairly readily be put right. Two or three examples may help to make clear what is meant. Modern Denmark offers a good illustration of social unity and freedom, with a culture that is truly "contemporary" in the sense of interpreting the civilization that exists, and an educational system which is vital and democratic. France on the eve of the Revolution, and Russia at the end of the Tsarist régime, both afford illustrations of a ruling class incapable of assimilating social change and of re-interpreting their tradition—that is to say, an obsolete culture. In both cases revolution was followed by the establishment of entirely new systems of education.

England in the nineteenth century also presents an example of obsolete culture, inasmuch as the pre-industrial classical and aristocratic tradition was not altogether successful in assimilating the Industrial Revolution, and the indigenous popular culture of pre-industrial England was lost in the new industrial towns. But the more significant thing about nineteenth-century England is the maintenance of a coherent national life, notwithstanding the strains and stresses within it, and the substantial approach in our own day towards a comprehensive system of education to the making of which all our cultural traditions have contributed. The power to contain variety within unity is one of the criteria of a community's health and vitality, and by that test English society stands high.

The statement that in a healthy society culture ought to represent the civilization that exists needs some qualification. Culture can be no mere photograph of civilization. There must always be a certain tension between culture and civilization; if it were not so, culture would be unnecessary and meaningless. Man must always strain in his thought and imagination beyond his achievements, and the tension between culture and civilization is the outward aspect of the inward tension in man which was discussed earlier. It was then pointed out that, in a sense, man must always repudiate nature since he belongs to two worlds, a natural world and (in a quite simple sense) a supernatural* world, and is forever challenged by the apparently insoluble problem of how to reconcile the claims of both. Man is both beast and god, and therefore cannot be a happy beast or a successful god. By

* The supernatural should not be confused with the unnatural.

the same token man both is within the historical process and also transcends the process. Man is the material of history and also the judge of history. That is why culture must be in tension with civilization, since culture, as well as being a picture of civilization, is also a judgment upon civilization. It follows that education can never be a mere matter of adaptation.

The aims of education cannot be discussed in general terms only. Principles must be interpreted in the context of actual situations, and particular programmes must be seen as interpretations of general aims. That is to say, education has both general and special aims. There are things which it is always the business of education to do; and there are the means by which these things have to be done in given circumstances. If the general aim alone is stated, we find ourselves presented with indubitable but useless truths. If only the special aim is stated, we have something practical but merely pragmatic and not related to first principles —i.e. not fully understood. If we are to frame a satisfactory philosophy of education it is therefore necessary to state a general aim and a special aim of education. Chapters II and III are concerned with a further examination of the general aim of education as already indicated in the preceding pages, and Chapter IV deals with the special educational needs of our modern western civilization.

II
The Personal

TWO formulæ were proposed in Chapter I to indicate the nature of education: (*a*) Education is the nurture of personal growth; (*b*) Education is an instrument for conserving, transmitting, and renewing culture. The next step is to examine the relation between these formulæ, the one being framed from the standpoint of individual growth (the microcosm) and the other from that of human history (the macrocosm), and to attempt a synthesis of the two. To that end it is necessary to consider further (in this and the following chapters) the nature of the personal and also the nature of the historical.

Self and Community

The term "personal" has already been used to indicate life at the rational and moral, rather than the merely instinctive, level. It is also clear that, in the full meaning that the word has gathered into itself during its long history,* "personal" implies both individuality and community. It implies individuality because we would not ascribe personality to the members of a primitive undifferentiated collective, such as a flock of birds, wheeling as one; that is to say, we do not believe that the unity of action is in that case due to the kind of intelligent and responsible individual decision which we associate with the personal.† It is this idea of personal responsibility that lies clearly behind the often quoted words of Sir Percy Nunn: "Nothing good enters into the human world except in and through the free activities of individual men and women."

But the "personal" also implies community, because no human being can come to his full personal stature in isolation. The

---

* See the interesting analysis of the origin and development of the word "person" in C. C. J. Webb: *God and Personality.*

† To say that personal behaviour must be intelligent and responsible is only another way of saying that it is rational and moral.

growth of personality is, in fact, essentially a social experience, and the higher activities of man, such as moral conduct, are meaningless apart from relations with other persons. The recognition of a relationship as one between persons is in fact the foundation of morality, because it means treating the other person as an end in himself, and therefore as having claims upon oneself, and not only as a means to some end of one's own. It is difficult, especially under the depersonalizing conditions of modern life when so many of our relationships are merely professional or official, to maintain the sense of the personal in our dealings with our fellow men. It is very easy to forget that the man behind the counter, from whom we get stamps or a pair of socks—and *a fortiori* the nameless civil servant who rejects our application for a permit—is a human being with a family and troubles like our own. But every time we forget that and allow him to become in our minds a *thing*—a piece of machinery or a piece of grit in the machinery—we are weakening the sense of community and undermining the foundations of morality.

Individuality and community, in the sense of the fulfilment of the self and the service of the common good, are both valid ends of conduct which, in actual experience, are always found to conflict more or less with each other but which, notwithstanding that universal experience of tension, man believes to be ideally reconcilable.

The tension between the claims of self and community is obviously related to the tension between the two-way urge, which is found in all living organisms, to get and to give—that is to say, on the one hand to attain and establish distinct identity and to feed the self with nourishment drawn from the environment, including other selves, and on the other hand to unite in the common life, merging the self and allowing its resources to be taken and used. This fundamental twin impulse of getting and giving, which Freud described as the ego- and sex-instincts, appears at first sight to be simply the subjective correlative of the claims of self and community. "Getting" is the assertion of the claims of self as a distinct individual, as against the rest of society, while the "giving" of the self in dedication to the common good is the acknowledgment of the over-riding claim of the community. But this neat correspondence between end and motive is too simple, and we have to recognize that there may be self-seeking motives for submission to the community and unselfish motives for assertion of self against the community. Greed for wealth and power are not the only motives of self-assertion. The martyr stands uncompromisingly against society because he is left with no other means of witnessing to some truth which the men of his generation need for their salvation but against which their senses are closed. Nor is public spirit the only motive for identifying oneself with the community. There is also the desire, springing from dread of isolation, for security at all levels from animal warmth to the comfort of shared beliefs and solidarity of opinion. The escape from isolation is also an escape from responsibility, and appeals not only to the loneliness of modern man but to his perplexity in an increasingly difficult world. Modern man's loneliness is clearly due to his loss of an assured place in a stable social structure and to his loss of conscious dependence upon eternal values sustaining the transitory world. That is to say, modern man has lost God and he has lost the full life of the pre-industrial local community. Modern social groupings are too unstable to afford any abiding sense of security, and modern problems are more and more bewildering. Little wonder that modern man is tempted to plunge into a neo-primitive kind of collective which relieves him of personal responsibility in return for an idolatrous devotion to the mass, the class, the party, or the dictator.

The dilemma in which man is placed by the cross-pull within him of getting and giving is made no easier by the complications that arise at the human level. At the animal level, as far as we can tell, the right balance of getting and giving is secured by instinctive response to stimulus, provided the appropriate environment is present. But at the level of conscious choice two developments contribute to give a perverse and paradoxical character to man's relations with his fellows. On the one hand the desire to get dominates over the desire to give. Getting seems to be the cardinal principle of life and it seems natural to man to rationalize his behaviour in terms of self-interest. Behaviour which is not obviously self-interested tends either to be interpreted as remote or extended self-interest (e.g. we treat other people decently in order to induce them to treat us in the same way) or to be ascribed to "instinct," as to something primitive and vestigial (e.g. maternal self-sacrifice). If those insects for whom the act of reproduction involves death could think, they would no doubt consider it as natural and reasonable to give their lives to make new life as it is to eat and drink. It is only civilized man who takes self-seeking for granted and finds it embarrassing to have to acknowledge and account for any other kinds of behaviour.

On the other hand, man also discovers that conscious efforts in the direction of self-seeking are strangely self-frustrating, that ambition costs us our friends, that power corrupts and wealth brings the curse of Midas, that "the pursuit of happiness was ever a most unhappy quest," that the secret of self-fulfilment is to lose oneself in something greater than oneself, and that the first condition of true freedom is to be liberated from self—from those fears and anxieties about one's own safety, comfort, and reputation which effectually inhibit full and creative action. "Whosoever would save his life shall lose it; and whosoever shall lose his life for my sake and the gospel's shall save it."* This is universal human experience and by no means limited to the Christian revelation. Socrates knew it and so did the Stoics. One of man's most ancient insights is into the creativeness of suffering and sacrifice, and the idea of life created through death is expressed in myth as early as 6000 B.C.† When Stanislavski said: "One must love art, not oneself in art,"‡ he was stating a principle which is true of life as a whole and which mankind has

---

* Mark viii. 35. Other versions appear in Matt. x. 39, xvi. 25; Luke ix. 24, xvii. 33; John xii. 25, which has the significant variant: "He that loveth his life loseth it." It is important to notice that, in all these gospel passages except one, it is not simply the losing of one's life that saves it but the losing of it in something greater.
† Cf. the death of Tammuz (the Faithful Son) and the mourning of his mother Ishtar (the prototype of the Mater Dolorosa), and the reappearance of the same myth in Osiris and Isis.
‡ *My Life in Art*, p. 298.

always known to be true, notwithstanding his perpetual failure to act upon it.

It is, then, the paradox of human life that man is ever tempted to make self his god and yet he knows all the time that the worship of self leads through frustration to destruction. He knows that the salvation of his soul lies in losing himself in something greater than himself which can liberate him for effective living; yet he finds self-love the hardest thing in the world to surrender. It haunts him even in his altruistic moments. "We have to ask ourselves," says John Macmurray:* "is it really the other person that I love, or is it myself? Do I enjoy him or do I enjoy myself in being with him? Is he just an instrument for keeping me pleased with myself, or do I feel his existence and his reality to be important in themselves?" The most fortunate people are those who are, so to speak, caught up unawares by an absorbing enthusiasm or consuming devotion so that self is forgotten before they stop to think whether the enterprise holds profit or loss. It would seem in fact that to *renounce* self is an impossibility; one can only be caught away from self. Which is only another way of saying that man cannot save himself; he can only be saved.

Returning to the rival claims of individual and community, we can see that the tension between them is felt both within the microcosm and in the macrocosm. In the microcosm the legitimate expression of individuality often conflicts with the controls exercised, perhaps equally legitimately, by the state. The conflict is obvious and dramatic in the case of cruelly persecuted minorities, but it is no less real in the case of the citizen who finds himself deprived by government regulation of liberties which his parents would have taken for granted. In the macrocosm the tension is between social systems that are individualist in principle and systems that are collectivist, and between individualistic and collectivist tendencies within the same system.

Love and Freedom

The central problem of social life, as it presents itself to the individual and to the community, is how to reconcile these rival

* *Reason and Emotion*, p. 32.

claims of self and society. A practical *modus vivendi* can usually be achieved by compromise; each individual agrees to concede certain rights to his fellows in order to induce them to make the like concessions to him. Duties are a *quid pro quo* for rights. In this way the individual is assured of a limited freedom and of adequate protection, and the community is assured of sufficient cohesion and stability while retaining enough variety and initiative within it to give it vitality. This sort of implicit social contract, which is the basis of every existing political community, allows of very great elasticity between extremes. But there are limits beyond which the system breaks down. Individual variety and initiative may be greater than the community can hold together in unity; the community will then disintegrate as the city states of the ancient world. Or the central power may impose itself so firmly, in the manner of an eastern despotism, that revolt is provoked or else initiative dies and the state becomes fossilized. In one case there is explosion; in the other desiccation. A good working test of the health of a community, as was suggested in another connection, is the power to contain maximum variety within unity.

Although this practical balance of liberty and control is the way in which the situation is in fact met by actual societies it is no real solution of the problem. It is no solution because it does not transcend the antithesis which gives rise to the problem; it only strikes a balance between the opposite poles of the antithesis. So far from being a solution, the usual working compromise between the claims of the individual and the claims of society is only a way of avoiding a solution.

At the philosophical level there are three possible answers to the problem of the rival claims of individual and society.

(i) We can say that the claim of the individual is alone valid. Self-interest is the only standard of conduct. If, as the Utilitarians maintained, the result of the universal pursuit of self-interest is in fact the welfare of all, well and good; but in any case there is no higher authority than self-interest.

(ii) We can say that the claim of society is alone valid. The state, as Aristotle said, is prior to the individual, who depends upon it for his very existence and owes it his total service. In its modern forms this doctrine likes to dramatize itself, as in the Hegelian mysticism of the state as a super-soul or the Marxian apocalypse of a new earth after the historical catastrophe.

Before going on to the third possible answer we ought to recognize that the terms "individual" and "society," which we have been using, are abstractions, often convenient but always treacherous. We are accustomed to the conventional picture of a hypothetical "individual" moving, like an actor on a stage, in front of a drop-scene called "society." Neither individual nor society exists in that sense. Individuals are neither separate nor self-sufficient. Society is neither a mere sum of individuals nor is it a super-ego, but is a complex of relationships of a kind to which the term "personal" is appropriate as indicating both the rational and moral nature of the association and also the fact that full human life is possible only in community.

(iii) The third philosophical position is that both sides of the paradox (the claim of the individual and the claim of the community) are valid, and the tension between them must be resolved by being transcended. This would be accomplished—theoretically—if we could find a principle that reconciles freedom and service; for the service that is perfect freedom would satisfy the claims of community and individual at the same time, since the individual would be able to fulfil himself in and through service to the community.

Freedom, it must be noted, is a positive thing—the achievement of something (i.e. the best of which one is capable) and not only the absence of something (i.e. restraint). It is true that absence of restraint is a necessary condition of freedom. But it is important not to confuse the conditions of freedom with freedom itself. We have already seen that the most fatal restraint from which we need to be liberated as a first condition of the achievement of freedom in a positive sense is the inhibition of self-love—i.e. anxiety and concern about one's own safety, comfort, or reputation. Without liberation from self, all other liberty is no more than a self-indulgent and ultimately frustrating escape from responsibility. One of the great weaknesses of our western liberal democracy is that its idea of freedom is of this negative sort. As the former President of the University of Chicago put it not long ago: "Our great preoccupation to-day is freedom. When we talk about freedom we usually mean freedom from something. Freedom of the press is freedom from censorship. . . . Freedom of thought is freedom from thinking. Freedom of worship is freedom from religion."*

We begin to approach true freedom in proportion as we lose ourselves in something greater than ourselves. We may expect, that is to say, to find freedom in service. But, while human experience at large endorses the paradox that service is freedom, it also clearly warns us that not any or every kind of service is liberating. The question therefore is: What kind of service is freedom? Or: What is the nature of the relationship in which service is freedom? Now it is clear that this relationship is what (to give it its best and shortest name) we know as love.† We know, from our own experience and from innumerable examples from history and everyday life around us, that devoted service liberates and fosters personal growth where unwilling service does not. But, having said that, we must obviously go farther. It is not enough to look at the situation one-sidedly. We have to ask not only whether the citizen, disciple, or devotee gives his service in love, but whether he himself is loved—that is, whether the person or institution he serves treats him as an end in himself and of infinite value as a human soul, or only as material or an instrument. If the latter, his devotion is misdirected and he will be destroyed like the moth in the flame. Not only that, but the person or institution served will ultimately destroy itself by accepting such service, since nothing is left in the end but ashes; the State that devours its citizens cannot be a community.‡ Only when the love relationship is, in modern jargon, bilateral is service really freedom, and the self given without reserve is

---

* Robert Maynard Hutchins: *Education for Freedom*, 1943. The Edward Douglass White Lectures at Louisiana State University, 1941.

† ἀγάπη not ἔρως.

‡ This does not, however, dispose of the important problem of what happens when the relationship is one-sided. Love then has powers of redemption which are more appropriately discussed in a later chapter.

given back fulfilled to the giver. That is the nature of love. And because that is the nature of love, it is a law of life that persons grow to full stature by giving, not by getting.

It follows therefore that the conditions of true freedom and also of true community are to be found in the context of the love relationship. It follows also that the key to true community is to be found in the meaning of the personal, since love is the essentially personal relationship. Love might in fact be defined as the relationship that treats people as persons—i.e. treats them as sacred. It is love that *constitutes* the personal: it is through loving and being loved that persons grow as persons.

The love relationship, though sometimes approached as between two or among a few persons, is never found in actual life except imperfectly. Institutions and associations do not love; for the most part institutions are not expressions of love so much as protective devices designed to make up for man's lack of love. We need the morality of law to supply the lack of a morality of love. But it is well that the morality of law should know its imperfection, for there is then some chance that love may work like leaven to redeem the morality of law.

But some institutions are more compatible than others with the principle of love. That is to say, some institutions do more to safeguard the ultimate sacredness of the individual human soul and go to utmost limits to protect minorities within a common life, while others ruthlessly exploit their human material in the interests of the line of policy determined by the group that holds power.

If this exposition is sound, we have arrived at the theoretical solution of the dilemma presented by the rival claims of individual and community, and we have arrived at it by nothing more sensational than the recognition of a truth constantly delivered through common human experience. It would seem that nothing remains except for mankind, in the clear light of reason, to make the command "Love one another" the foundation-stone of social life and proceed to build upon it. It is notable, however, that after six thousand years of civilized history, man still fails to achieve the community of love, evident as is its charm, not to say expediency. Human beings continue to precipitate themselves into ever larger and more terrible catastrophes rather than treat one another decently. This persistent sinning against the light suggests on the face of it that virtue is not, as Socrates maintained in the *Protagoras*, a function of reason, but that, in the language of the Collect for the First Sunday after Epiphany, it is one thing "to perceive and know what things we ought to do," but another thing to "have grace and power faithfully to fulfil the same."*

It was said a little earlier that persons grow as persons by loving and being loved. Paradoxical as it may seem, the "being loved" is in an important sense prior to the "loving." In other words, man needs redemption. The paradox becomes clearer if we ask: Why cannot man resolve his central dilemma of his own volition, in the light of reason? Animals do so by instinct. Why does man make such a mess of it with his superior equipment? The answer is that man makes a mess of it *because* of his superior equipment. For animals, conflict is resolved by the adjustment of exterior relations. For man the conflict remains in the soul. The reason for this is clear. The two fundamental urges that need reconciliation—(whether, with Freud, we label them self and sex, or separation and union, getting and giving)— these two urges come into irreconcilable conflict when they become *conscious*. At the level of consciousness self-love is born. When some other impulse comes into conflict with the urge to self-preservation, man *knows* it. Instead of the animals' emergency machinery of self-preservation man has a sentiment of self-interest which makes him anxious when he ought to be bold, greedy when he ought to be generous, which in other words makes him constantly mindful of self when effective action demands that he should forget self. It is thus man's self-conscious reason which creates man's central problem. Man is justly

* Socrates, asked whether virtue can be taught, held that virtue depends on knowledge and therefore can be taught, since knowledge can be taught. Modern psychology agrees with the Christian view in its estimate of the importance of the emotions in behaviour.

crowned Lord of Creation, but his crown is a crown of thorns, pricking blood all the time from his brow.* There are three recognized ways in which the inhibition of self-concern can be broken and the constrained power liberated. One is the violent stimulation, at instinctive level, of some great primary urge, such as the mother's urge to defend her young, so that it temporarily overwhelms everything else and dominates the situation.† The second is Dutch courage—i.e. the anæsthetization of the higher centres by something like alcohol so that the person becomes an extreme extrovert. Under the influence of drink we are able to forget ourselves literally as well as metaphorically. The remaining means is the condition in which a person's whole being is so claimed and taken possession of by some supreme enthusiasm that concern about self is lost in devotion to the object. It is obvious that this third alternative is the only one of the three which, by accomplishing the reorientation of the person as a whole, offers a solution at a mature level. But—and this is very important—the object of devotion must irresistibly appeal to the person. Notwithstanding the legend of Pygmalion one cannot create or constitute the object of devotion and then decide to be swept off one's feet by it. One must be taken out of oneself and lose oneself. It is in this sense that the "being loved" is prior to the "loving," and that man needs to be redeemed.‡

The Role of Psychology

Before leaving this discussion of the personal in relation to freedom and community we ought to pay some attention to the claims of psychology to solve man's problems and give him

* In the words of Geoffrey Farjeon's song "Beasts of Prey," sung by Elisabeth Welch in the review *Tuppence Coloured*, "Man is the Lord of the Universe. He knows much better but he does much worse." Cf. St. Paul's words in *Romans* vii. 19: "The good that I would I do not and the evil that I would not that I do."

† It is possible to become so selfish that even these "natural" appeals provoke no response.

‡ Cf. man's need of salvation, page 14 and Chap. vii *passim*. The philosopher Bosanquet was really making the same point when he said: "One can make a beautiful thing or a true proposition; but one cannot make a thing beautiful or a proposition true." Beauty, Truth, and Goodness claim us. We do not constitute them; we can only respond to them.

control of his destiny. One cannot be acquainted with the magnificent work of the psychologists in the field of education alone, especially in remedial work, without gaining a deep sense of our debt to these workers and their art. The cheap sneer at psychology can only come from ignorance and stupidity. But we do no service to a good thing by claiming too much for it. There is no hostility to psychology in suggesting that its role is something more modest than to make man master of his fate.

It is a favourite thesis with writers on education to recognize modern man's tensions and sense of frustration, to draw our attention to the indubitable fact that if man behaved more rationally he would behave better, and then to claim that the self-knowledge attainable through the practice of psychology would enable him to direct his behaviour in the light of reason.

If there is any truth in the general argument of this chapter, it should follow that man cannot expect to add cubits to his stature by taking thought, though an understanding of the working of his own mind ought to help him to take the kinks out of himself which make his stature appear less than it really is. Or, to put it differently, psychology ought to enable man to make the best of himself, though it contains no magic to make that self better. The intrinsic conflicts and problems of man's nature, which make him "Nature's mistake," or God's mystery, remain when psychology has done its best. Psychology does not alter the fact, if it is a fact, that man is a creature that needs redemption. The proper function of psychology is to help him to understand himself and to place himself, so to speak, in the path of redemption—to teach him how to expose himself to grace. But psychology, being itself simply one of man's own techniques, will not redeem him, any more than a knowledge of the physics of solar radiation will keep him warm.

To say that psychology will not redeem man is not to say anything disrespectful about psychology. It is rather to deny the dogma of human self-sufficiency which dominates modern thinking but which has nothing to do with psychology except to pervert its development. The notion that mental techniques (any more than industrial techniques) can accomplish human salvation has about as much to do with the legitimate development of psychology as the search for the philosopher's stone had to do with the early development of chemistry—that is to say, it provides a highly dubious incentive.

It is worth appreciating that the dogma of human self-sufficiency, carried to its logical conclusion, leads not to the morality based on reason for which most modern writers plead, but to no morality at all. In this connection the recent William Alanson White Memorial Lectures by Dr. G. Brock Chisholm* are of special interest. His thesis is a very clear example of the modern uneasiness about the state of our civilization coupled with the tenacious belief that human techniques† can put right what millenniums of civilized history have put wrong. His claim that we must eradicate the concept of right and wrong is perfectly logical. For if we postulate human self-sufficiency we are logically committed to the condemnation of that sense in man which tells man that he is *not* self-sufficient. That is to say, we must condemn the sense of sin. This is easily accomplished (and in this Dr. Chisholm only adopts common contemporary practice) by confusing the sense of sin with the sense of guilt, thus presenting opposites as synonymous and obscuring the fact that the sense of guilt is natural man's resentment against the sense of sin and his desire to rid himself of the *sense* of sin without doing anything about sin itself. Guilt is a morbid condition which psychology can help to resolve; but man remains "in

* *The Psychiatry of Enduring Peace and Social Progress* by Dr. G. Brock Chisholm, C.B.E., M.D., William Alanson White Memorial Lectures given in October, 1945, and published in *Psychiatry*, February, 1946, by the William Alanson White Psychiatric Foundation, D.C. Briefly the steps of the argument are—(i) We are the kind of people who fight wars every fifteen or twenty years. Very few people benefit. Therefore why do we do it? (ii) The root of the trouble in human nature is morality. Therefore we must get rid of morality. (iii) The ultimate responsibility for changing human nature and thus preventing war rests upon the psychiatrists.

† Speaking in New York in May, 1947, as Executive Secretary of the World Health Organization about the forthcoming International Congress on Mental Health, Dr. Chisholm referred to "the planned development of a new kind of human being, one who can live at peace with himself and his fellow men."

sin" so long as he indulges the illusion of self-sufficiency, for the sense of sin is essentially the recognition of that conflict in man as a creature at odds with himself and needing at-one-ment. For a being perfectly at one with himself and with the universe there would of course be no need for morality and no meaning in the concept of right and wrong, just as the law can have no meaning for one who has attained perfect freedom. But it scarcely follows that the denial of morality is the *recipe* for putting man at one with himself and the universe.

These William Alanson White Lectures have been referred to because they perfectly present the logical necessity for denying morality if we assume human self-sufficiency. Thus Dr. Chisholm speaks of "the re-interpretation and eventual eradication of the concept of right and wrong which has been the basis of child training, the substitution of intelligent thinking for faith in the certainties of old people" as the aims of psychotherapy. Nevertheless, to do Dr. Chisholm justice it must be pointed out that his illustrations make it clear that what he is really attacking is not morality at all but prejudice, which is related to morality in much the same way as guilt is to sin. It is not really possible for man to deny the concept of right and wrong any more than he can deny the concept of true and false or beautiful and ugly. These are categories of man's distinctive humanity and they hang together. If one of them is pushed out of one door it comes in again by another. The denial of morality in practice only amounts to the claim that conduct ought to be guided by reason rather than prejudice—an unexceptionable contention if there ever was one. Nevertheless it is highly significant that the assumption of human self-sufficiency *logically* involves denial of the sense of sin and the concept of right and wrong, and we should be grateful to anyone who makes that clear. The fact that modern man's central dogma has this implication, while at the same time it is impossible for man to deny his sense of sin without denying his humanity, is at least circumstantial evidence against the dogma.

III
The Historical

THE nature of the personal was discussed in the last chapter. Before we can satisfactorily formulate the general aim of education, it is necessary to examine also the nature of the historical. In other words, having looked at man's problems in terms of the microcosm we must look at these problems in terms of the macrocosm.

Man and Time

"The communion of saints," wrote Professor A. N. Whitehead, "is a great and inspiring assemblage, but it has only one possible hall of meeting, and that is the present." There is a sense in which Aeschylus and Shakespeare, Plato and Hegel, Abelard and Karl Barth, Cabot and Scott are all contemporaries. The world's masterpieces and great adventures belong to all time; they cannot be contained in the footsteps of the years but take wing into eternity. It is less obvious, but perhaps even more important, that what is true of the great figure and the great achievement is true of all human life. Man is both within the time process and outside it, both immanent and transcendent. From one point of view he is bound by the chain of events. Yet from another point of view he has a freedom from the time process which as far as we know the animals do not enjoy, because he does not live only in the moment. He transcends the time process by virtue of being able to think about it and to relate events to one another in ways quite different from their chronological sequence. He can see the time process as it were from above, and to that extent he can act upon it from above. That is to say, he can act not only under the immediate stimulus of events but in the light of knowledge and imagination and with reference to ultimate considerations. Since man's transcendence of the time process is a function of his self-conscious reason, it is a function of the personal, and provides one measure of personal living. In truly personal behaviour action ensues upon a total and rational evaluation of the situation, and is not determined from moment to moment by external impacts. Man has to live in the stream of time, but he need not be at the mercy of its currents.

History is possible because man transcends time. At first sight this may seem a paradox. But reflection will show that if human life were wholly absorbed in the time process there would in fact be no history. The creatures of instinct are presumably so absorbed, and they have no history. They have a biological cycle, which endlessly repeats itself, and some of them have elaborate civilizations, which never change. History is essentially dramatic in character, a unique and irreversible development, with plot and counterplot, tensions and crises. Man alone has history. And history is man's struggle, amplified to the scale of the macrocosm, to solve the problems that arise from his distinctive humanity. History arises therefore from the tension between man's immanence in the time process and his transcendence of it. It is by virtue of his transcendence of the time process that man can conceive the possibility of acting upon the process, of manipulating it; and history is man's effort to control and direct the stream of events. The mere acceptance of the stream of events —i.e. total absorption in the time process—cannot give rise to history. Nor could total transcendence of the process, for in that case there would be no sequence of events. It is the dual existence of man that gives rise to the "agony," in the strict sense of that word, which is history.

The tension between man's immanence and his transcendence is also the tension between the actual and the ideal, between what is and what man conceives ought to be. Now it is clear that, so long as history goes on, there can be no resolution of that tension. Or, to put it differently, if the tension were to be resolved, history would come to an end. It is true that we cannot conceive the "end" of history any more than we can conceive the complete fulfilment of our Utopian dreams. But if these dreams came true, history would not need to go on, for it would, so to speak, have done its job. An apocalyptic conclusion, supervening like the New Jerusalem upon the convulsive termination of the course of history, is in fact a normal accompaniment of Utopian programmes. That there is a certain flavour of anticlimax about these visionary havens beyond the storm is to be expected, since man is a creature of storm and stress, and, though he yearns for the peace of fulfilment, he is unable to picture anything but the struggle.* Nevertheless, the struggle is meaningless except as related to fulfilment; and the need for fulfilment is an essential element in man's historical experience.

There is no reason to believe that man collectively is master of his fate any more than man individually. At least two considerations point to the contrary. Human society is made up of persons and, *a priori*, we have no right to postulate any capacity in society collectively which has no foundation in persons. Viewed empirically on the other hand, human society presents no evidence of being able to redeem itself. History is eloquent of noble struggle, it is true, but also of continual and most varied frustration, so that man's fundamental problems change their form without achieving solution. If there is any maintained progress in civilization it is an increase of potentiality for *both* good *and* evil, not an advance towards good or evil. The fact that from time to time man has collectively *believed* in a progressive approach to perfection, or has comforted himself with the hope that perfection, so long elusive, lies just round the corner of some technical discovery, tells us more about man's desires than about the nature of history.† In default of reason or evidence to the contrary, it would appear that collective man is under the same limitations as individual man—i.e. that in both cases the will to fulfilment meets with frustration, from which

* That is why pictures of heaven have always been so much less convincing than pictures of hell. Readers may recall the anonymous rhyme—

> The burning at first
> Will no doubt be the worst,
>   But time will the suffering soften;
> While those that are bored
> By praising the Lord
>   Will be more so by doing it often.

† A century ago we believed in progress. To-day we rather desperately clutch at techniques, as we are solemnly bidden to trust in physical science or psychology.

some kind of rescue is needed. In other words, the macrocosm as well as the microcosm needs redemption. The one is the large-scale projection of the other. Whether any redemption is available at either level is another matter.

Incarnation

Our historical thinking depends on our assumptions about the relation of Reality to the time process. Broadly speaking there are three possible views upon which ultimately depend our attitude towards social change, the relation of the ideal to the actual, and the relation of the individual to society.

(i) *That Reality is Wholly Transcendent.* Truth, as Socrates believed, is to be found only beyond the transitory world of space and time, in the sphere of the eternal. History only faintly mirrors Reality and in the last analysis is without significance. In Berdyaev's words, the Greek philosophers "had no conception of history as fulfilling itself." Man must seek liberation from the flux of history and the implications of the material world and can find perfection only in a changeless state outside space and time. Eastern mysticism carries this view to the limits of negation.

(ii) *That Reality is Wholly Immanent.* The opposite to the absolutist view is thorough-going relativism. In this view, represented by Croce and Collingwood, there is no reality transcending the historical process. As Croce put it: "Reality is history and is only historically known." It is a view that liberates us from the transcendental at the cost of extinguishing all standards of value external to the process. Man has to take up one of two attitudes. He may say that there is no ultimate meaning in anything, and that he must make the best of human existence in a universe which is not interested in man; this attitude may be optimistic or pessimistic, ethical (Stoic) or hedonistic (Epicurean). Or he may, so to speak, set up the process itself as an absolute so that values are all one with the process. The Marxian view that there are no criteria except the accomplishment of the social revolution is the natural consequence of identifying reality with the historical process and denying all reality external to the process.

(iii) *That Reality is Both Transcendent and Immanent.* Of the two preceding views, one releases man from history and the other releases him from the transcendental. In both cases what is left means nothing. For the absolutist the historical process, in which after all man is immersed, is illusory. For the relativist what is is right, or there is no right at all; i.e. there are no abiding norms by which the process can be interpreted. In neither case is there any Judgment of history.

In the third view Reality is both transcendent and immanent. History is to be taken seriously not only as a true revelation of reality but as a mode of creation (or as *the* mode of creation as far as we are concerned). Yet the full meaning of history lies beyond history, and so do the norms of conduct. Reality fills history but is not contained by history. There are universal values by which history is judged and there is a dialectic of time and eternity. This view has all the difficulties of paradox; but it affirms the reality of history and at the same time the reality of ultimate values.

The earliest clear appearance of this "incarnational" view of reality is in the Old Testament. The Hebrews were the great empiricists of the ancient world* and the first to grasp the reality of history. "The most representative Hellenic thinkers," wrote Berdyaev,† "conceived creation as something static, as a sort of classical contemplation of a well-ordered cosmos. . . . It was the Jews who contributed the concept of 'historical' to world history. . . . Christianity introduced historical dynamism and the extraordinary force of historical movement. . . . The dynamism introduced by Christianity derived from its idea of the immediacy and uniqueness of events which was foreign to the pagan world." For the Hebrews, God was ever active in history, and for the prophet God spoke in and through the turmoil of social and political events. This is a view of the revelation of truth in striking contrast with Plato's.

The Hebrew insight is still recognizable, though pantheistically transformed, in Hegel's doctrine of the Spirit struggling into

---

* Cf. their interest in prophylaxis.
† *The Meaning of History*, pp. 27–28, 33.

being through history. Hegel's view parts company from the Hebrew-Christian tradition inasmuch as it gives intrinsic status to man as an expression of the divine, and does away with any need for redemption. Marx inverted Hegelianism so that, instead of history being the expression of the Idea, the Idea is the product of the historical process. By thus denying original reality to anything outside the historical process itself, Marxism really lines up with thorough-going relativism, which allows no values transcending the process.*

If there is anything in the argument of the previous chapter it should follow that this incarnational view of history squares with experience. It squares, that is to say, with the view that man is both inside and outside the historical process, that his freedom lies in his transcendence of the time process, and that he can be truly personal only in so far as he transcends the historical.

This question of the relation between the universal and historical aspects of experience can perhaps be made clearer by means of an illustration, and the best illustration can probably be found in the field of art. We should all agree that a work of art (a statue, a painting, or a piece of music) can and should be understood in terms of its historical development. That is to say, we can understand the work of art better if we know something of the historical conditions which induced the painter to make use of a certain style, or the musical composer to develop his theme on certain lines. We can, for example, understand the development of the novel better if we take account of the growing instability of the social system, and the growth of modern psychology. Similarly, to take an even more obvious example,

* We are not here concerned with the merits of individual philosophies of history. But it is worth noting the relation in which Marxism stands to Hegelianism. Marx inverted Hegel's idealism, in which the process was the externalization of the Idea, and gave us a materialism, in which the Idea is the internalization of the process. Like Croce, Marx got rid of the transcendental by bringing the whole of reality within the historical process (which therefore becomes amoral since there is nothing beyond history to judge history). But, unlike Croce, Marx does not leave it at that. Being concerned fundamentally not with philosophizing but with salvation, Marx must bring the transcendental back again, and does so in the only way he could—by means of an Apocalypse. The classless society comes down from heaven like the New Jerusalem.

the development of photography played an important part in turning pictorial art away from literal representation towards things that the camera cannot do.

At the same time a work of art can never be reduced to purely historical terms, for in that case it would cease to be art and would simply become the resultant of certain conditioning factors.* A work of art has a universal quality and validity which transcends the sequence of historical cause and effect which led up to it, and it is this transcendent value which in fact constitutes it a work of art. From the point of view of its universal and eternal quality, the historical circumstances of its production are irrelevant.

The importance of this illustration lies in the fact that what is true of a work of art is also true of human experience in general. If a work of art only truly becomes a work of art inasmuch as it transcends the historical process, so also a person is only fully a person by virtue of transcending history. So long as a person is considered only in terms of historical conditioning he is nothing but a group of factors. Everything is historically conditioned, and there is no escaping the "agony" of history. No one knew that better than the Hebrew prophets. But the full meaning of everything is to be found in its transcendence of history. To make use of the language of the Fourth Gospel, there is no meaning or value in the Logos becoming flesh unless He is also

* The absurdity of the purely historical interpretation is made clear in the following passage from the Edward Douglass White Lectures for 1941 by the then President of the University of Chicago (Robert Maynard Hutchins: *Education for Freedom*, 1943, pp. 32-3): "The methods of disposing of philosophy by placing it in a certain time and then saying that time is gone been adequately dealt with by a contemporary historian. He says, 'it ascribes the birth of Aristotelianism to the fact that Aristotle was a Greek and a pagan, living in a society based on slavery, four centuries before Christ; it also explains the revival of Aristotelianism in the thirteenth century by the fact that St. Thomas Aquinas was an Italian, a Christian, and even a monk, living in a feudal society, whose political and economic structure was widely different from that of the fourth-century Greece; and it accounts equally well for the Aristotelianism of J. Maritain, who is French, a layman, and living in the bourgeois society of a nineteenth-century republic. Conversely, since they were living in the same times and the same places, just as Aristotle should have held the same philosophy as Plato, so Abelard and St. Bernard, St. Bonaventure and St. Thomas Aquinas, Descartes and Gassendi, all these men, who flatly contradicted one another, should have said more or less the same things.' "

the eternal Logos. Continuously involved in history as he is, man can never identify himself with, or be wholly absorbed in, history.

The view of history which has been described as "incarnational" also accounts for the reflection in the macrocosm of the tension already observed in the microcosm; that is to say, it accounts for the restlessness and frustration of history. The rise and fall of civilizations and systems, the recurrence of revolution, the perpetual defeat of man's efforts towards perfection, must be seen not as accidental and unaccountable features of history but as possessing the same primary significance as the frustration within the individual personality. Every gain in history is accompanied by some loss, every reforming revolution by the irrevocable destruction of some real values. If there is any law of progress, the progress is an increase of potentiality for both good and evil and not any total advance towards the better or the worse.

The thesis that historical development is towards increasing tension between possibilities of good and possibilities of evil is obviously illustrated by the technical progress that marks modern civilization and, less obviously, by the dilemma of modern man whicih Erich Fromm discusses in his book *The Fear of Freedom*. The enormous technical achievements of the last few centuries have not made man master of his fate, but have in some ways put him even more at the mercy of the natural forces that he has learnt how to control. It is interesting to note that A. J. Toynbee takes the view that high technical achievement is connected with the decline rather than with the growth of civilizations. If we relate our remarkable technical progress with our equally remarkable loss of conviction about ultimate values and purposes, we have almost a definition of decadence. In the field of art we recognize decadence in the elaboration of technique together with poverty of meaning—i.e. preoccupation with form rather than content—just as, in the primitive, we recognize the opposite characters of rich and vigorous meaning and crudity or naiveté of expression. Primitive art has plenty to say but says it imperfectly; decadent art has a sophisticated mastery of expression but little worth saying. What is true of art appears also to be true of civilization as a whole.

Erich Fromm in *The Fear of Freedom* is concerned with the dilemma created by the emergence of the individual, in modern history, from the limiting securities of pre-individualistic society. The emancipation of modern man from the old authorities, political, economic, intellectual, has not brought him inward freedom, but rather perplexity and fear. He is afraid of the new insecurity and isolation, and finds himself confronted by two alternatives. One, the easier, is to escape from the tension by means of a new and ultimately destructive submission to the totalitarian state. The other, and much harder, way is to go forward to the realization of positive freedom by entering into the spontaneity of true fellowship. "The familiar picture of man in the last centuries was one of at rational being whose actions were determined by his self-interest and the ability to act according to it. . . . The more the middle class succeeded in breaking down the power of the former political or religious rulers, the more men succeeded in mastering nature, and the more millions of individuals became economically independent, the more did one come to believe in a rational world and in man as an essentially rational being. The dark and diabolical forces of man's nature were relegated to the Middle Ages and to still earlier periods of history, and they were explained by lack of knowledge or by the cunning schemes of deceitful kings and priests."* But this optimism based on reason and self-interest was not justified in the event. "Modern man, freed from the bonds of pre-individualistic society, which simultaneously gave him security and limited him, has not gained freedom in the positive sense of the realization of his individual self; that is, the expression of his intellectual, emotional, and sensuous potentialities. Freedom, though it has brought him independence and rationality, has made him isolated and, thereby, anxious and powerless. This isolation is unbearable and the alternatives he is confronted with are either to escape from the burden of this freedom into new dependencies and submission, or to advance

* *The Fear of Freedom*, p. 5.

to the full realization of positive freedom which is based upon
the uniqueness and individuality of man."* "Man, the more he
gains freedom in the sense of emerging from the original oneness
with man and nature and the more he becomes an 'individual,'
has no choice but to unite himself with the world in the spontaneity of love and productive work or else to seek a kind of
security by such ties with the world as destroy his freedom and
the integrity of his individual self."†

Relativism

The modern western mind is not interested in the absolute, and
modern views of history mostly take the form of some kind of
relativism. "The effects of evolutionary theory," writes A. L.
Rowse, " . . . have been such as completely to recast our view
of the universe, of man and his place in it. . . . It has had the
effect of undermining the absolute claims of religion and metaphysics, of ethics and law. . . . The evolutionary view of the
universe has brought us to an almost completely relativist way
of looking at things. . . . Some people seem to think that the
study of history, the whole concept of history, was revolutionized
under the influence of ideas worked out, notably by Darwin,
in the field of natural science. R. G. Collingwood thinks on the
other hand that evolutionary ideas in science were developed
under the impact of history. . . . In fact, evolutionary theory
in science and what has been called, modestly and sensibly in
England, 'the historical method' (historismus, or historicism, in
Germany) are twin developments of the same fundamental
movement in thought, which characterizes the 'mental climate'
of the nineteenth century. Bury saw that clearly. 'The growth
of historical study in the nineteenth century has been determined
and characterized by the same general principle which has
underlain the simultaneous developments of the study of nature,
namely the *genetic* idea. . . . For history it meant that the
present condition of the human race is simply and strictly the
result of a causal series (or set of causal series)—a continuous

* *Ibid.*, p. x.
† *Ibid.*, p. 18.

succession of changes, where each state arises causally out of the preceding'."*

There is nothing wrong with the historical method as such; it is in fact indispensable. Only good can come from the use of evolutionary categories in our interpretation of social development. The trouble comes when, as is too often the case, the genetic process is taken as the *only* dimension of reality—when man is thought of as being totally immersed in the process and his transcendence of the process is forgotten. The view of man as being wholly enclosed in the process has certain important consequences which are worth noting.

To begin with, the identification of man with his history leads to the assumption that man's eternal problems (e.g. the reconciliation of the claims of individual and society) can be solved *historically*—that is, by arriving at the right stage of historical development. Now the evolution of fresh phases of civilization and culture often clearly is, and in one sense must always be, the historically "inevitable" result of the failure of the preceding phases. From this point of view failure is the only conceivable reason for historical change; Utopias are necessarily final. But there is no reason to suppose that one stage of historical development rather than another will accomplish man's perennial aspirations. It is one thing to say that the social revolution and the dictatorship of the proletariat is the necessary result of the failure of capitalism. But it is quite another thing to expect the dictatorship of the proletariat to inaugurate the perfect society. In other words the redemption of a social order is not the same thing as the replacement of one stage of development by another. The passage from one stage of development to another changes the idiom in which man's eternal problems present themselves. *Plus ça change, plus c'est la même chose.* There is no reason to expect any stage to be final. History will "end" when it does not

* A. L. Rowse: *The Use of History*, pp. 115–119. In what follows, "history" and "historical" are in most cases used to denote this way of looking at human behaviour as a stream of events. There is an inevitable ambiguity about the use of the word "history," which may mean either the substance of human development in time or man's way of observing that development. Where in this chapter the word is used in the former sense, the context should make this clear.

need to go on—i.e. when a particular phase has been fully redeemed. Theoretically this redemption might happen at any stage in history, if people were wise and good enough. For it is persons and not systems that are redeemed, and change of system is the recurrent evidence of the failure of persons. Practically, there is no particular reason to expect the redemption of human society to happen as a result of the socialist revolution or of any other change of system. It is one thing to see a revolution as a judgment on the failure of a régime; it is quite another thing to see in it the salvation of society.

The identification of man with his history and the refusal to recognize reality outside the historical dimension also lead, naturally, if not necessarily, to a deterministic philosophy of history. The importance of this aspect of the general theme of this chapter justifies a fairly full discussion of it.

The familiar problem of "determinism" and "free will" is often confused by being stated in the form of an antithesis between radical determinism (i.e. the doctrine that choice is accounted for without remainder as the result of past events) and radical indeterminism (i.e. the doctrine that choice is entirely uncaused action). Neither of these radical views is tenable. Radical indeterminism is as meaningless as motion in an infinite vacuum. Radical determinism, while not in the same sense meaningless, has the fatal implication that our acceptance of it must itself be determined—that is to say, if we believe it, we do so not because it is true but because we are conditioned to believe it.

All behaviour is determined in the sense that it is response to some "given" situation. There are many things that we cannot choose, whether because of external limiting conditions or because of limitations in ourselves. It is important to recognize the fact that the constitution of the self is among the "given" elements. But to acknowledge this is not to deny the reality of choice.*

It has been pointed out that the limitations imposed by

---

* "Our constitution is put in our own power." "It is not motives that act, but persons who act in virtue of their motives." A. E. Taylor: "Freedom and Personality." *Philosophy*, July, 1939.

circumstances and our own constitutions are *per se* limitations of the range of choice rather than of the power of choice. It is one thing to be faced with only two alternatives; it is another thing to be incapable of deciding between them.

Before going on to inquire what is the basis of the human power of choice it is as well to observe that the power of choice is itself the ground of moral responsibility. It is because man acts with intention that there can be any meaning in holding him responsible. "Where there is no intention there is, properly speaking, no act, but only the happening of an event."* Conversely, man could be relieved from responsibility if it could be shown that he never acts with intention. Moreover, we must recognize that moral responsibility includes responsibility for what we ourselves become. Whatever may be the factors limiting and conditioning our behaviour, choice is not merely the disclosure of a preconditioned preference, but is an act through which we make and change ourselves. Decision not only discloses what the self is but makes the self what it will be.

Reference has already been made† to the human power of transcending the stream of events. Man transcends the time process by virtue of being able to think about it and relate events to one another in ways other than their chronological sequence. And by virtue of this transcendence of the time process man can conceive the possibility of acting upon the process; history is the outcome of man's efforts to manipulate events. Now this transcendence (which Professor A. L. Reid calls "detachment" and Professor A. E. Taylor called "Reason") is the basis of the power of choice. In Taylor's words: "Reason or intelligence is in its very nature a principle of indetermination in each of us. There is plainly a sense in which the possession of rationality implies absence of complete determinism."‡ And he goes on to argue that a rational creature is never completely amenable to suggestion or other pressures, but responds to a situation with assent or refusal "according as he sees reason." The more rational he is the more he will look at all sides of a question before deciding, and

* *Ibid.*   † See pp. 25, 26.   ‡ *Ibid.*

in so doing demonstrates that he remains undetermined in respect of the situation up to the point of decision. Since logical sequence has nothing to do with time sequence, and logic does not belong to impersonal "nature," our acceptance of a logical argument is not the product of a sequence of natural events. As Professor A. L. Reid puts it, "a cause of action which is a reason is different from a cause which is a natural event," and the first cannot be explained away in terms of the second.

It is by virtue of the power to transcend the stream of events that the self can act as a coherent whole, in relation to a situation as a whole, summoning all resources of knowledge and imagination, making the action his own, taking full responsibility for it—acting, that is to say, as a person. Such behaviour is to be contrasted with behaviour at the instinctive level, where action is apparently determined in a quasi-reflex manner by immediate stimuli. In the first type of behaviour we recognize personal volition; in the other case we see a creature of impulse. Our possession of rational freedom, however, does not mean that we always exercise it, nor even that the power to exercise it remains unimpaired. The power of choice, inseparable as it is from personal responsibility, needs to be educated as do other faculties. We can lose the power of choice through abdication or disuse. Our business is to cultivate it by exercise.

Freedom ensues, therefore, in proportion as the self transcends the stream of events, acting as a whole in relation to the situation as a whole. But—and this is important to what follows—the stream of events is still there, and it remains possible to take a merely behaviourist view of what we see. If we look at the piece of behaviour as it were from the outside, stimulus and response are all that we shall see. A behaviourist or "determinist" psychology *must* result if we adopt a standpoint which excludes any other. Writing of Kant's postulate of free will, C. C. J. Webb says: "Yet an act, as an event in time, cannot *look* free, when surveyed from without, either by others than the doer, or by the doer himself after the act is done. Like any other event, it must have antecedents, among which the same principle as elsewhere governs our scientific study of events constrains us to

38

search for a cause and, even though we do not succeed in finding it, to assume it to be there. As *phenomena*, then, our actions are determined, even though they are done—and could only be done —under the idea of freedom."*

If we look at human behaviour as a stream of events, a stream of events is what we shall see. That is to say, we shall see groups of factors impinging on each other, and, in so far as we interpret *post hoc* as *propter hoc*, we shall observe sequences of cause-and-effect,† in which antecedent events are "causes" and subsequent events are "effects." This method of "accounting for" events is always incomplete, but—so long as we look at things in this way, as phenomena—there is nothing to tell us that the method is *necessarily* incomplete; within the limits of the method we are entitled to assume that, if we were in possession of all the facts, we should be able to demonstrate completely the dependence of every event upon every antecedent event. ‡

The result of viewing behaviour as a stream of events is the same whether we are considering the activity of an individual or the movements of history. In the one case we shall be interested in such factors as qualities of character (e.g. the meticulous diligence of Hobbes), bodily health (e.g. Judge Jeffreys' suffering from the stone), early educative influences (e.g. James I's hatred

* C. C. J. Webb: *A History of Philosophy*, pp. 166-7.

† We need not, in this connection, concern ourselves with the question of the nature of determination in the material world as compared with the nature of determination in the mental world. It is worth reminding ourselves, however, that we know nothing about "causation" in the material world and that our common way of thinking about it is fairly obviously derived by analogy from mental experience.

‡ It is not necessary, for the present purpose, to answer the question whether the determinateness of any event could ever be completely demonstrated. There is, it is true, an irreducible alogical element in experience which makes its complete rationalization impossible. If that were not so, there would be no difference between the unique, irreversible sequence of events which is history and the universalized pattern of relationships which is science. And it would seem that this alogical element is due to that very transcendence of the stream of events which is the quality of human experience *par excellence* but which the "historical" standpoint excludes from view. For our immediate purpose the present argument holds good if we *suppose* a complete demonstration of determinateness to be possible. It would still be true that what is "inevitable" when seen in one dimension is volitional, or "free," when seen in the other dimension.

of the Presbyterians), general cultural tradition (e.g. the religious heritage of Dante or Milton). In the other case we shall take account of political and administrative conditions (such as the growth of the House of Commons when the Crown's hereditary revenues had become insufficient for government, or the breakdown of the financial system of eighteenth-century France), economic factors (such as the need for overseas markets for an industrially expanding country), and physical conditions (such as the steep and stony valleys of Greece, conducive to city states and olive-growing). In either case, and in all the interpenetration of the two, we are dealing with groups of factors, and the kind of determination that we shall be in a position to demonstrate is the determination of subsequent events by antecedent events. Whether or not we attribute historical effects to personal volition will depend on the schools of psychology and philosophy to which we belong. But—and this is the important thing—if we do admit acts of volition, they can appear only in their outwardness as events—externalized as factors along with the rest, taking their place in the pattern of determination at the *vis-a-tergo* level —and not in their inwardness as acts transcending the stream of events.

Viewed from the standpoint which it is generally agreed is the one proper to the historian, human behaviour must appear, therefore, as a course of events in which the mode of determination is that kind of *vis-a-tergo* impact which we usually describe as "cause-and-effect." We see human behaviour from the outside and not from within, and we therefore cannot, within the limits of this view, become aware of that wholeness of action in which we recognize freedom and which can be known only in the inwardness of personal experience. Thus, to the historian .*qua* historian, a work of art does not appear as an æsthetic experience. The historian is not concerned to evaluate, or even to recognize, the beauty of architecture, or the truth of philosphy. In fact he has no means, *as historian*, of doing so. His business is to explain, in terms of conditioning factors, why the architect built as he did and why the philosopher thought as he did, and to show the influence of those kinds of building and thinking upon subsequent events. To enter into the work of art as beauty, or the philosophy as truth, it is necessary also to enter the transcendent inwardness of personal experience and activity. For the work of art can be understood only as personal creation; it is the personal quality of the activity that makes it art. When we say colloquially that an artist put his whole soul into his work we are saying something quite literally true. Art is the affirmation of the free self acting as a totality. The same is true of all activity, whether intellectual or moral, which has this quality of identification between the activity and the person, so that he says, as it were: "This is myself. I authenticate it and take full responsibility for it." If a man were to attain the fully personal level in all things, his whole life would have this quality which we recognize in a work of art. Whether we "explain" the artist in terms of his art or *vice versa* is of no consequence. The important thing is their identity. The same is true of the prophet and his message. The man is his vision and the vision is the man. We can say that the man explains the vision or the vision explains the man. At that level there is no other explanation, and, either way, the creative activity, as such, escapes the historian. In one sense St. Paul's life was determined by his vision of God. In another sense, or at another level, it was determined by a group of conditioning factors, social, educational, temperamental, and so on, which the psychologist and historian can usefully analyse. Both "explanations" have their validity at their own levels, but they are not equivalent or convertible the one into the other;* the conditioning factors will not add up to the vision of God, nor can the vision of God be reduced to a group of conditioning factors.

The bearing of all this upon the question of historical determinism should now be clear. The question whether human action is "free" or "determined" is not a question about the

---

* The attempt to explain away some achievement of the human spirit as being "nothing but" the historical factors that can be shown to have led up to it is known as the "reductionist fallacy." A familiar example is the presentation of mature religion as a mere elaboration and sophistication of primitive superstition.

nature of history itself, but rather about the standpoint from which it is observed—whether human behaviour is seen in its externals or in its inwardness. If we look at the process externally, it is seen as a causally related sequence of events which appear the more inevitable the more complete the picture becomes. The more detail we can fill in, the more we can eliminate chance and explain away choice. If Queen Anne had not had a contracted pelvis, the Hanoverians would not have come to England; and no doubt the right kind of physiological knowledge would show that the shape of Queen Anne's pelvis was no more accidental than the weather. And so with mental factors. We must not forget St. Augustine's Œdipus complex. As to economics, we have long been taught to look in this field for the efficient springs of human action. Thus the key to the spread of Christianity is to be found in the condition of the proletariat of the Roman Empire.

If we could put all the different factors together so as to have complete knowledge of the antecedents of an event, we should have established the inevitability of that event. Both chance and choice would have disappeared. Now it is important to recognize that this thesis is quite valid within its own limits, and that, at its own level of truth, it is no less true of individual activities than of the collective "movements" of history, no less of artistic achievements than of political events, of thought than of action. There is a sense in which Wolfe's capture of Quebec and Gray's composition of the *Elegy* were both equally inevitable.

The trouble comes when man's transcendence of the time-process is denied or ignored. For when man is identified with the process, the "historical" order of reality becomes the only reality, and "historical" truth the only truth.

A determinist view of history, therefore, is not a discovery about the nature of history, but is simply the result of viewing the process in a certain way, just as a silhouette is not a revelation about the real nature of a solid object but is its appearance when viewed in a certain light. The observers of history in its externality are in the same sort of position as the watchers in Plato's cave. Viewed inwardly, human action is seen in terms of personal decision and therefore free. Viewed externally each event is the consequence of preceding events. It is nothing other than this paradox that Tolstoy was expressing when he said: "Nothing is inevitable until it has happened. Everything appears to have been inevitable once it has happened."

The denial of all reality transcending the historical process also means the denial of moral and personal values, since there is nothing by which the process can be judged except the apparent direction of the process. What is historically necessary must be right. There can be no ethics but expediency and persons must be subordinated to process. There are no rights pertaining to human beings as such, who cease to be ends in themselves. Rights pertain only to the beneficiaries of successive phases of social change; thus, for example, the liquidated retain no rights against the revolution.*

The dilemma in which the modern mind finds itself in this matter of man's relation to history is well illustrated by the attempt made by A. L. Rowse in *The Use of History* to reconcile universal values with historical relativism. Referring to the effect of evolutionary theory in undermining the absolute claims of religion, metaphysics, ethics, and law, he asks: "Are we reduced to a complete historical scepticism?"† He then considers two separable problems, and in each case his answer is interesting.

Having shown the connection between evolutionary thinking and the historical determinism of Marx, he seeks to resolve the contradiction between the apparent inevitability of the historical process and the apparent freedom of personal choice. Mr. Rowse answers the question by saying that "it depends whether you mean by history the surface stream of events . . . or whether you mean by it the deep underlying tides and currents."‡ The

---

* Speaking at a meeting of the Social Committee of the General Assembly of the United Nations, the Soviet Delegate, Professor Alexei Pavlov was reported as having opposed the proposition in the projected United Nations Declaration of Human Rights that "all human beings are born free and equal in dignity and rights" on the grounds that "Freedom and equality in rights are not inherent by birth, but are a product of social structure." *News Chronicle*, 12th October, 1948.

† *The Use of History*, p. 122.   ‡ *Ibid.*, pp. 130-1.

surface story "is capable of infinite variation," while the underlying story is "profoundly conditioned."* This answer is really
no answer since it begs the question of the relation between the
surface story and the underlying story. Unless we are told what
this relation is—e.g. whether the surface variations possess any
real, or only an apparent, independence—the question remains
exactly where it was. What Mr. Rowse does not recognize is
that the historical process becomes inevitable the moment we
deny reality transcending the process. The real answer to the
question is that it depends whether we view events in their
externality as phenomena or inwardly in terms of personal
experience and decision.

It is true that the inevitability of historical events is more
apparent in the case of collective behaviour than in cases of
individual action, and this lends plausibility to the view that the
deep currents are "determined" and the superficial agitations are
"free." That is doubtless why the exponents of historical determinism prefer to deal in "movements." Thus, in Lord Acton's
words, Buckle "made the individual soul of no account in his
investigations on the history of human progress. . . . Hence
not individual acts, but their statistics, engage his attention."
Thus Bury, speaking of "the conception of human history as a
continuous, genetic, causal process—a conception that has
revolutionized historical research and made it scientific," points
out that "the predominant importance of the masses was the
assumption which made it possible to apply evolutionary principles to history . . . for it is only when the masses are moved
into the foreground that regularity, uniformity, and law can be
conceived as applicable." But, although the inevitability of
history is more easily thought of and more convincingly demon-
strable in the case of collective movements, we should not allow
ourselves to be misled into thinking that movements are determined and men are free, when the truth is that men and movements are equally determined when viewed in a certain way—
that, if we knew all the factors, social, economic, psychological,
metabolic, and so on, that conditioned their production, we

* *Ibid.*, p. 128.

should recognize the works of Shakespeare as being no less inevitable than the Industrial Revolution.

The other problem that Mr. Rowse considers is the effect of historical relativism in destroying moral value. He rightly says that "origin is not the same thing as validity, nor is knowledge of the origin the same thing as judgment of it."* That is to say, he sees that experience has universal value as well as historical significance,† but he does not see that, by saying that, he has re-admitted the transcendent. He affirms the reality of our belief that hatred and cruelty are evil and love and forgiveness are good. These values are not merely relative to circumstance. But, being a good modern, he does not want the transcendent, and tries to keep it out of the picture by insisting that "those (permanent) values emerge from, and rest upon, the positive experience of man in history."‡ He does not see that he is begging the question because man's experience in fact transcends history. If these values are independent of the time-element they stand to that extent outside history and do not wholly "arise out of" history, though history repeatedly testifies to them. In other words man himself is in one sense within history and in another sense beyond history.

History and the Personal

It is by living at the personal level that man transcends the time process. But there is nothing automatic about this transcendence. Always potentially capable of personal living, by virtue of his rational and moral consciousness, man achieves personal stature painfully and imperfectly. It is only in proportion as man does approximate to full personal stature that he can expect to be master of himself and of history. The less personal human life is, the less transcendence of the time process there can be. In other words, the more completely man is immersed in the process, the more true a deterministic interpretation of history becomes. A society based on a deterministic ideology could go a long

* *Ibid.*, p. 149.
† "It is obvious that everything has an historical aspect. But that does not mean that history *is* everything." *Ibid.*, p. 148.
‡ *Ibid.*, p. 155.

way to making its ideology come true in fact by encouraging behaviour at the level of mass activity rather than of personal responsibility. In such a society the masses would be more or less blindly immersed in, and therefore subject to, the process of cause and effect, while the ruling group would be living on the advantage that the process happened to bring to them. History can afford examples of this kind of society, the possibilities of which are the more sinister in a world that works better if most people are like machines Berdyaev, speaking of the historical tendency towards externalization, pictures a conflict between man and history in which man was never so much at the mercy of the process of history as now. "Man faces the threat that nothing shall be left of himself, of his personal and intimate life, no freedom of his spiritual life or his creative thought. He is submerged in large collectives, subject to non-human commandments. It is demanded of man that he give himself up without reserve to society, the state, the race, the class, the nation."*

The extent to which the categories of cause-and-effect, rather than of responsible decision, are adequate as a total account of the history of a human society depends therefore upon the extent to which the members of the society achieve personal living. This reflection gives added significance to the opinion, referred to earlier, that the most serious danger to which our civilization is exposed is the undermining of personal values. For it means that a world in which persons are less valued will become a world in which persons play less part in determining events—a world, in fact, which is depersonalized in the profoundest sense.

A fuller review of the contemporary world will be made in the following chapter. For the present purpose it is enough to note the increasing tension in modern western civilization between technological development on the one hand and human bewilderment on the other. "What shall it profit a man if he gain the whole world and lose his own soul?" It is clear that the supreme need of the modern world is for the maintenance of personal values and the creation of personal living. Any attempt to achieve the truly personal level in living and thinking must

* *The Fate of Man in the Modern World*, pp. 12–13.

also be an attempt to create true freedom and true community. There is no need to recapitulate previous arguments. It is enough to recall that true freedom and true community are two sides of the same thing, since freedom is to be found in the service of a community in which persons are treated as ends and not as means.

Freedom in Community

We are now in a position to state the general aim of education as the creation of personal freedom in community. The examination of the personal in Chapter II led to the conclusion that persons are fulfilled in liberating service, though man is prone to seek fulfilment in ways that prove frustrating and destructive. The examination of the historical in Chapter III threw more light on the nature of the personal, in its relation to the time-process; whence follows the conclusion that personal values are tied up with what was called an "incarnational" view of history, in which the historical process is conceived neither as a mere shadow of reality nor as the whole of reality, but as the true and creative revelation of reality. The argument of both chapters disclosed a state of tension in the heart of man and in civilization, the two pictures being reflections of each other. The tension in civilization between individualism and collectivism reflects the conflict between self-interest and true fulfilment in service and between responsible decision and escapist submergence in a group. The individual's inability to square his superior human powers with his need of "redemption" is reflected in the paradox of the disintegration of the structure of thought and belief amidst unprecedented technological achievement. Whether we consider the microcosm or the macrocosm it is clear that the tension can only be resolved by the creation of spontaneous fellowship, or love. A discussion of the ultimate conditions of the creation of fellowship belongs to the second part of this book. Meanwhile a fuller analysis of the present state of our civilization is necessary in order that we may be able to interpret the general aim of education in terms of the particular problems and conditions of our age.

IV
Education for Our Time

IN ONE sense the problems of education, as of human society as a whole, are always the same; in another sense they are always changing. There is no such thing as "a good education," if by that is meant an education that is good for all times and places. The education of the medieval knight and of the eighteenth-century gentleman were good for their purposes—far more adequate, for that matter, than the secondary education of to-day is to the more exacting needs of modern democracy. It is necessary not only to state the universal aims of education but also to interpret these principles in the idiom of the contemporary situation. By coming to life in the needs of our present world, a general philosophy takes on the quality of *tua res agitur*.

We have already seen that in our own age the problem of the relation of the individual to the community has acquired a new acuteness—that a characteristic of our time is the increase of tension in both microcosm and macrocosm. We must now examine the historical development of this situation in order to see in proper perspective the special task of education in the modern world.

The Character of Our Age

We appear to be witnessing the disintegration of a civilization—a civilization remarkable both for progress in techniques and for decay of belief, for increased control of means and loss of conviction about ends. A disintegrating civilization is naturally reflected in a demoralized culture, and our cultural history during the last few centuries has certain features which we must grasp if we are to understand our present problems.

At the level of symptoms, perhaps the most obvious indication of cultural decline is the lack of any true popular culture of the industrial age. The most serious social result of industrialization has been the uprooting of people from their indigenous cultural heritage,* and the failure to evolve anything adequate in its place. At all social levels, our pre-industrial culture failed to assimilate the Industrial Revolution. The popular culture that had enriched Shakespeare's England was destroyed. The classical, literary tradition of polite culture survived but was unable to come to terms with science and technology, with the result that there is no coherent culture of the scientific and industrial age, comparable with the medieval world view; and, in the absence of any such unity, we observe the aggravation of several false antitheses such as the cleavage between the "liberal" and "vocational" principles in education and the rival claims of Arts and Science to provide the material of a liberal education. Our learned culture is to a great extent atrophied, though it retains a good deal of prestige value and still supplies much of the material of the schools and universities. In default of a true popular culture, the mass of the people—so long denied opportunity for profitable recreation—have readily accepted a sham† culture of which the cinema is the most powerful single vehicle.

Since we have neither a unified view of life in which our knowledge and ideas all find their place, nor a live cultural tradition in which all sections of the community share, it follows that we have no adequate cultural interpretation of our contemporary world. Our culture is too incoherent and fragmentary to give us spiritual or even intellectual mastery of our situation.

One reason for the lack of a true culture is that the Industrial Revolution destroyed the old social relationships based on neighbourhood and substituted new social divisions based on economic function. In the sixteenth or eighteenth century, while the learned and aristocratic culture was the reserve of a minority, there was nevertheless a common national heritage of songs, games, country lore, and so on, which was shared by all and in terms of which people of different social status were bound together in the life of the local community. One of the strongest

---

* Including, in H. A. L. Fisher's phrase, "the natural piety of the soil."
† Sham, because it is on the whole escapist rather than interpretative.

social bonds—perhaps the strongest—was religion. And for many generations in England the common knowledge of the Bible was a real factor in creating community. It is no doubt easy to exaggerate the amount of knowledge of the Bible that was actually to be found in any section of the population. But there is no doubt that the Bible was much better known than it is to-day. Nor can there be any doubt that, apart from religious considerations as such, no other literature can better give ordinary folks, whatever their station, a deep insight into the meaning of life. It is interesting to notice the emphasis that Berdyaev lays on religion as a social bond. "Religion was the meeting-place of the masses with the aristocratic culture. Only religion is capable of making such a combination: neither philosophy nor science, nor enlightenment, neither art nor literature can do this. Deprived of religious basis, any high and qualitative culture inevitably becomes separated from popular life and an isolated cultural elite is produced, which keenly feels its uselessness to the people."*

Industrialization has destroyed the mixed local community, and has given us the slum, the suburb, and the municipal housing estate. There is no longer a common cultural heritage, religious or secular.† If the pre-industrial aristocratic culture failed to assimilate the Industrial Revolution, Protestantism failed to assimilate the change from free competition to public control. In an age of free competition "self-help" was the appropriate economic principle, and fitted with the Puritan ethic which gave nineteenth-century religion in England most of its strength. In an age of public control the centre of gravity has shifted from personal to social morality; as a people we have become more critical of unethical attitudes towards the community and easier

---

* *The Fate of Man in the Modern World*, p. 114.
† It might with some truth be claimed that, notwithstanding the natural antagonism of capital and labour, there is also a natural affinity between all those engaged in industry, such as to make the industrial world into a community with its own standards, integrity and loyalties, the members of which understand one another much better than any of them understand people who have no experience of industrial life. This view contains enough truth to supply a corrective to any simple analysis of society in terms of class conflict. But it is doubtful whether those engaged in modern industry have ever formed a community comparable with the village. They neither live in the same neighbourhood nor share the same recreations.

in our judgment of private morality. In the field of public morality the Puritan ethic gave little help. In spite of important movements within the Churches—notably the Christian Socialism of Kingsley and F. D. Maurice—institutional Christianity in the nineteenth century was not strong enough to assimilate the changes in the social order and re-interpret morality, or to assimilate science and re-interpret doctrine. Consequently religious authority weakened and conduct partly broke loose from any kind of moral control and partly discovered a new obligation to the state. "In the Twentieth Century," writes Professor G. M. Trevelyan, "self-discipline and self-reliance are somewhat less in evidence, and a quasi-religious demand for social salvation through State action has taken the place of older and more personal creeds."*

The failure of the pre-industrial culture to respond to the challenge of industrialization and of institutional Christianity to respond to the challenge of public control are manifestations of the failure of a whole social order to assimilate social change and adapt itself to new conditions. The failure in this country was far from complete, and, as has been pointed out in a previous chapter, the most significant thing about the history of England in the last century or so is the extent to which a coherent national life has been maintained in spite of the stresses and strains within it. But the question for us to-day is no longer whether England can solve her problems. National problems can no longer be separated from world problems, and we are concerned no longer with English solutions merely but with world solutions. It is important therefore for us to become more fully aware than we have been of tendencies in western civilization as a whole. The great and inevitable expansion of the State's activities and the new relation of the individual to the State have disclosed and aggravated a contradiction which cleaves through the whole of modern society.

The contradiction springs from the affirmation of the individual in the Renaissance and Reformation, which has resulted in the change (to use the famous phrase of Sir Henry Maine's) "from

* *English Social History*, p. 510.

status to contract." Liberated from the old authorities, mental and social, modern man found himself free to pursue not only truth and beauty wherever he might find them, but wealth also. He had a free and equal right to compete with his fellows in the open market. Herein lay the great contradiction. Theoretically the freedom of competition was complete. In practice, since the race can never start from scratch—in fact, there is no "scratch"— the liberty of some inevitably means the enslavement of others. The dilemma is sometimes expressed by making a distinction between political democracy (whose slogan is: One man one vote!) and economic democracy (whose slogan is: Workers of the world, Unite!).

Modern western society thus presents a contradiction between theoretical political equality (the equal right of every man to get what he can in a competitive world) and actual economic inequality (resulting from that competition). Moreover, the self-interest of the successful is to retain a competitive society, though they are continually forced to make concessions to the "have-nots," partly because the ideal basis of society is increasingly acknowledged to be democratic and partly because technical development requires a more educated people. Meanwhile the self-interest of the less successful is on the side of the publicly controlled society which progressively emerges. The tension increases as it becomes clearer that the publicly controlled, or "planned," society is the only possible kind of society under modern conditions, the alternative to it being not competition but chaos. This inevitability of the planned society in turn raises with a new acuteness the old question of individual free-dom—not only the freedom of the industrialist or financier (the adventurer vis-à-vis the community) but the freedom of the individual citizen (the human being vis-à-vis the state). This problem of freedom in the planned society* is in fact the central problem of our age. It is obvious enough that we can no longer expect to do what we like. Whether we shall be able to like what we do is another matter. It is significant that Sir Stafford Cripps

* The theme of Sir Fred Clarke's *Freedom in the Educative Society*. U.L.P 1948.

not long ago said that the supreme test of democracy is whether people can do the right thing of their own accord.

The central contradiction in modern society exists both in the macrocosm, as a tension between the "haves" and the "have-nots," and also in the microcosm, as a tension between the individual and the state. In both spheres the tension increases, so that in our own time the situation has become nothing less than a crisis of civilization.

The emergence of the individual at the time of the Renaissance, and the liberation from the old authorities, is the secret of the dynamic character of modern civilization. Political democracy and scientific progress are both consequences of this Discovery of Man. But the emancipation of the individual is the secret also of the failure of our civilization, inasmuch as modern man has failed to create community at the conscious and intelligent level which man's new status requires. Once man claims individual responsibility, or has it thrust upon him, his social relations must be at a rational and moral (i.e. a fully personal) level; mere instinct, mere habit, mere expediency, no longer afford a foundation for community. By affirming his individuality man necessarily makes the problem of community a more difficult one by raising it on to a higher plane.

The failure of modern individualized man to create community accounts for his loneliness and bewilderment. Never has man been more lonely than among the crowded populations of industrial cities; never so bewildered as amidst the tremendous achievements of science. From this loneliness and bewilderment, from the intellectual and moral anarchy of a world with no stable values, man seeks to escape in one of two directions.

One way of escape is the homeopathic one of individualism, which disposes of responsibility by denying it, and takes a negative view of freedom as the absence of control, thus confusing the condition of freedom with freedom itself. Individualism is more interested in liberty of choice than in what is chosen, and in means than in ends, since ends of any kind lay claims upon us and recall us to some kind of responsibility. This preoccupation with means, to the neglect of ends, which characterizes a degenerate liberalism, is illustrated in the field of education by the impressive development of educational techniques during the present century* and the weakening of our convictions about the ultimate purpose of education. We are inclined to avert uncomfortable questions about educational aims by saying that we want to produce, not people adapted to a given environment, but people of maximal adaptability.

Taken to its limits individualism means the negation of community and of all claims upon individual independence. In the last resort it is anarchy. It is obvious, of course, that economic individualism is impossible, and all political parties now acknowledge this. What is less obvious, perhaps, is that intellectual anarchy has gone much farther in our liberal western society than economic anarchy could go without producing disintegration. There is no longer any embracing view of life, no cultural unity in which the parts find their place and meaning. Instead, our culture presents a number of separate fields of thought and action, each a law unto itself, with its own norms or no norms at all. It is a state of affairs that is conducive to the development of techniques and separate bodies of knowledge; but, among all the specialists, no one is anxious to shoulder the responsibility of saying what the accumulation of knowledge and proliferation of techniques really *means*. Philosophy, which of all branches of knowledge might be expected to offer comprehensive interpretation and reveal meaning, occupies itself increasingly with problems of method rather than of content. In the absence of any accepted world-view or ultimate criteria, no truth can claim more than a relative validity. This chaos of values is the most serious feature of our present crisis; for when intellectual and moral values drift, man himself loses personal stature. The disintegration of the world-view inevitably involves the disintegration of the personal; the breaking-up of thought and knowledge into separate systems means also the dissolution of man himself into a group of functions.

---

* I do not intend to depreciate the value of techniques in themselves. But we ought to be concerned with ultimate values in education as well as with the measurement of I.Q.'s.

The alternative to the negation of community is the perversion of community. In this direction the escape from the responsibilities of being an individual is effected quite simply by total surrender to the state, or the party, or some other collective. The individual is presented with a clear-cut objective and his duty is clearly prescribed. He has no choice and virtually no private life.* The ultimate annihilation of personality is not only inevitable but an object of policy, since depersonalized human beings are easier material in the hands of a ruling group. The temptation to escape from all other problems by total immersion in the mass is one which young people especially, with their capacity for enthusiasm and loyalty, find it difficult to resist. But they are likely to experience some misgivings before long. "A section of the young," writes Martin Buber, "is beginning to feel to-day that, because of their absorption by the collective, something important and irreplaceable is lost to them—personal responsibility for life and the world. These young people, it is true, do not yet realize that their blind devotion to the collective, e.g. to a party, was not a genuine act of their personal life; they do not realize that it sprang, rather, from the fear of being left, in this age of confusion, to rely on themselves, on a self which no longer receives its direction from eternal values. Thus they do not yet realize that their devotion was fed on the unconscious desire to have responsibility removed from them by an authority in which they believe or want to believe. They do not yet realize that this devotion was an escape. . . . But they are beginning to notice that he who no longer, with his whole being, decides what he does or does not, and assumes responsibility for it, becomes sterile in soul. And a sterile soul soon ceases to be a soul."†

As between the negation of community (individualism) and the perversion of community (collectivism) there may seem to be little to choose. Two things, however, are worth pointing out. One is that individualism at least postulates liberty, though

* Cf. the law passed by the Czechoslovak Parliament in October, 1948, which gives the government power to act in cases of "subjective guilt."
† Martin Buber: *Between Man and Man*, p. 115.

it may fail to create freedom; and liberty implies the possibility of experiment and variety in thought and action. The other is that, when individualism and collectivism come into conflict, collectivism is likely to prevail, at least for a time, since a perversion is stronger, because more positive, than a negation.

Clearly the only salvation from the Scylla and Charybdis of chaos and collectivism, false freedom and false community, is in the community of free fellowship. Impossible of achievement as this ideal may be, the practical aim of democracy is to provide such a combination of liberty and order as is most conducive to the development of the community of freedom and responsibility. The historic tradition of Britain, in which liberty and order are both held sacred,* makes this country peculiarly fitted for the task of demonstrating to the world a practical approximation to the essential democracy, in which people do the right thing of their own accord. This is plainly the role for which Britain is cast, and it may not be too late for her to play this part among the nations if she will take her destiny seriously and discipline herself for it.

The Special Aim of Education To-day

Man needs society, but, under actual conditions of imperfection, he must defend himself against society. The tension between man and society was never so acute as it is to-day. Never was the redemption of personal values so desperately necessary in a world that denies them. Herein is the special educational urgency of the contemporary situation—the special aim of education for our time, and the special opportunity of a nation that knows how to combine liberty and order. The aim is nothing less than a double redemption, of the individual and of society—of the

---

* Among the great nations there is probably none in which the average man is at once so law-abiding and so independent; and there is certainly none which has contributed so much during the centuries to the idea that liberty and order are two aspects of the same thing. The control of feudalism, the establishment of an efficient civil service under the Tudors, the establishment of the power of the Commons in the seventeenth century, the quiet accomplishment of a social revolution by means of parliamentary reform in the nineteenth century, the development of a full system of social services in our own century by a remarkable combination of public authority and voluntary initiative—these are some of the chapters in the story of a unique political achievement.

bewildered individual from depersonalization and of the planned society from tyranny.

The practical meaning of this proposition will be clearer if we look at some of its implications, in which education can help us.

(i) We need to gain a faith by which to live—a faith, that is to say, which is both adequate as meaning and efficacious for action. The prevailing intellectual and moral relativism of our time is rotting the roots of deep conviction from which alone personal life can grow. Our liberal western culture is very conscious to-day that its existence is threatened by forces which ought to be resisted. But the greatest weakness of liberalism is not its doubt about its *power* to resist; it is the dawning doubt about its *right* to resist—that is to say, the inkling of its spiritual and moral bankruptcy.* A discussion of the nature and sources of an adequate faith belongs to the second part of this book. For the moment it is enough to remind ourselves that no true education can escape the responsibility of communicating a view of life—that is, of "indoctrinating." The cult of the open mind is a way of camouflaging the poverty of an education which has no view of life to communicate. Indoctrination is not an educational crime; it is an educational necessity, in religion as in table manners. The crime is to indoctrinate in such a way as to destroy the freedom and responsibility of the pupil. It is by no means impossible—and the world's greatest teachers from Socrates onwards have proved it to be the very heart of teaching—to present a strongly held faith in such a way as to challenge the beholder to come to terms with it on his own personal responsibility. That there is no necessary opposition between doctrine and freedom is clear when personal freedom is at the very heart of the doctrine.

(ii) We need to make efforts to understand our world and our place in it. This kind of understanding is the more needful in a

* This point is clearly implied in a leading article in the *News Chronicle* (2nd November, 1948) on the war in China. After referring to the corruption of the Nationalist régime and the failure to make reform the condition of aid to the Kuomintang, the article goes on: "It is incumbent upon us to do all that can be done to save China from Soviet domination. But we shall have neither the right nor the power to do anything at all if we cannot find and support Chinese leaders who stand for the values in which we ourselves believe."

civilization which is increasingly complicated and of which the controls are remote and invisible. Here the historical approach is surely the right one. The most valuable result of the study of history is the habit of looking at situations in the perspective of their development. Historical study sets us free from the limitations of our place and time; it helps us to distinguish the universal and the permanent from the local and the transitory, and makes us conscious and critical of those basic assumptions which form the groundwork of culture and which, by being taken for granted by one group and ignored by another, are a fruitful source of misunderstanding between people. The best cure for prejudice is to see how it arose.

An historical understanding of our world is likely to yield two other results of special value at the present time. One is a truer and more imaginative sense of vocation, springing from an appreciation of the place of particular occupations in the scheme of things. The other is a more enlightened attitude towards the authority of the state—an attitude which recognizes that the extension of public services both enlarges and restricts freedom, and that compulsion is a relative term, depending on the degree of intelligent co-operation between the citizen and the government. Such an attitude will at least rise above certain crudities, such as the notion that there is a simple alternative between liberty and governmental control or a simple opposition of individual *versus* government; or the converse notion that there can be a simple identity between government and the interests of a particular group.

(iii) We need to recover the sense of vocation which is too easily lost in a civilization where most people's jobs are of a kind to which the term vocation can scarcely be applied without irony. In any society people need three things: a job, by which they earn their daily bread; a vocation, which is a means of self-fulfilment through service to the community; and leisure, in which they can relax the special tensions of their work and re-create themselves. There are always a few people (such as some university professors who are paid to pursue their hobbies) for whom these three things are identical; whether they are really blessed in their lot is perhaps open to question. There are many more—and these are the fortunate ones—for whom the first two are the same; their job is a vocation. But the great mass of people in an industrial society have jobs which, though useful to the community, cannot by any stretch of the imagination be called self-fulfilling. Such are the repetitive bench-jobs in factories, most of which can be learnt in a few hours, and also many clerical jobs.

The solution of this problem of the job that does not contain the makings of a vocation is not easy to see. Conceivably the further development of technology will eliminate these occupations in which human beings are in fact supplying the incompleteness of the machine; but that solution cannot be assumed, and in any case it would seem to contain fresh difficulties of its own. Something no doubt can and should be done through education to help people to grasp imaginatively the meaning and importance of their own contribution to the whole industry or the whole nation. The dullest occupation and the humblest process become great and inspiring when understood in their total relations. But if we are to be realistic we must recognize the limitations of what we can hope to achieve in this way. It is no doubt a romantic and philosophical thought that the raging storm and the refreshing shower are both made up of drops of water. But if one were a drop of water one would probably find life equally dull either way. One must not confuse standpoints, nor allow ideas about education for citizenship to become sentimentalized.

More could perhaps be done to give workers more share in the management of industry and thus more sense of responsibility. But the practical difficulty, in this as well as in other fields, is that large-scale organization tends to make democracy unreal. A more hopeful approach to the problem may be to seek ways in which opportunities for vocation can be found for people whose jobs do not offer sufficient scope. That is to say, if the job is not a vocation, vocation must be found elsewhere. In this connection we are bound to think of the possibilities of all kinds of voluntary activity—possibilities which have as yet been scarcely explored. The Civil Defence services during the war gave us a glimpse of the ways in which responsibility brings opportunity of personal development to many whose jobs are limited in scope. If we can take the hints offered by Civil Defence and by the best voluntary social activities such as Women's Institutes and Young Farmers' Clubs, together with the possibilities of adult education (including intelligent entertainment as well as systematic study), we may begin to imagine the cultural life of a neighbourhood, essentially democratic, growing spontaneously through voluntary activity, and rooted all the time in real, felt needs. If we can re-create a richer spontaneous neighbourhood life, we shall have found the secret of the creation of a true contemporary culture. If not, life will become still more depersonalized as we perform our unthinking jobs and passively submit to being looked after and amused. The modern penetration of the state into every field of human activity is no doubt necessary; but it carries with it dangers from which human society can only be rescued by the development of voluntary initiative not only alongside but within systems of public administration.*

(iv) We need to recover the meaning and importance of the family, and education can help us to do so by spreading knowledge about family life and home-making, by setting the highest possible standards in these things and by building up the status of the housewife, and by promoting such activities as can engage the activity of families as such.† The most important thing of all, perhaps, is to get society at large to take the housewife's job seriously as one that calls for much specialized knowledge in varied fields, much skill, and great personal qualities.

The family, and not the individual, is the real unit of society. The family, because it is the primary community, is the natural

---

* The following extract from the Editorial comments in *The Times Educational Supplement* for 6th November, 1948, is interesting in this connection: "The board of governors is the way chosen for associating the local community with the school in its midst. These boards, if manned by the right people, can become most valuable social instruments—a sphere in which responsibility can be borne by ordinary people for matters of great importance, in a period when the general tendency is to remove responsibility from ordinary hands."

† E.g. Community Centres of the Peckham Health Centre type.

context in which personal values are learnt and the meaning of personal living understood. It is in the family that relations are essentially personal, and each person is valued *as* a person. The integrity of the family is moreover the most important bulwark against the destruction of personal values by other forces in the modern state.

Wherever the state seeks to make itself omnipotent it attacks the family. In this country there has been no direct attempt to weaken the family; and in fact there are some signs of the opposite intention.* Nevertheless, a number of factors have contributed to weaken the strength and coherence of the family. Universal education not only removed what had been a very important parental responsibility but also operated to enlarge the cultural gap between generations. Old-age pensions and state provision for age and sickness have diminished the family's responsibility for its weaker members, while in general the extension of social services has substituted impersonal public provision for personal private provision. Economic changes have broken down the old-fashioned continuity of occupation from father to son; the tendency is for members of a family—and often all grown members at that—to scatter in different employments, and the weekly pay-packet disregards all family implications.† The multiplication of public recreations has drawn the members of a family out of the home, and the housing shortage has driven them out. The result is that the members of a family may scarcely meet from one end of the week to the other.

The increased difficulties of family life are at the same time a challenge. The housewife's vocation is a much more difficult one than it used to be, not only because of the complications of rationing and shortages, but because much higher standards of knowledge are called for in fields ranging from dietetics to

* E.g. Family Allowances, extension of benefits of the new Social Insurance scheme to housewives without additional contribution, provisions of the Children Act, 1948.

† It is possible that the high domestic standards and general morale of mining villages owe something to the fact of common employment and the tradition that women do not go out to work.

psychology. The coherence of the family depends less on authority and convention, and the success of family life depends more directly on personal qualities than in days gone by. Family life under modern conditions, rightly viewed, can therefore be a stimulus to the development of the best in personal relations.

The Character of Modern Western Education

Our age has been described as one in which mastery of techniques has been developed at the expense of conviction about ultimate meaning and purpose. If that is the character of our world, it is not remarkable if our education exhibits a preoccupation with means rather than with ends.

The most serious weakness of modern education is the uncertainty about its aims. A glance over history reminds us that the most vital and effective systems of education have envisaged their objectives quite concretely, in terms of personal qualities and social situations. Spartan, Feudal, Jesuit, Nazi, Communist educations have had this in common, they knew what they wanted to do and believed in it. By contrast, education in the liberal democracies is distressingly nebulous in its aims. We appreciate the need for intelligent and responsible citizens in a democracy. And we acknowledge an ethical tradition which is broadly speaking Christian though somewhat diluted. But our sense of purpose in education is weakened by our uncertainty about the ultimate grounds of those values in which we think we believe. If we are none too sure what we believe, we are still less sure why we believe it. That doubt about ultimate foundations takes away from our confidence in those values (such as the Four Freedoms) which we still assume to be held by all.

Liberalism is right in believing that neither truth nor the liberty and responsibility of the individual to seek truth ought to be subordinated to political or any other kind of expediency; but liberalism is wrong in tolerating the lack of a common faith. The problem for liberalism is thus stated in the Report of the Harvard Committee on *General Education in a Free Society*: "The ideal of free inquiry is a precious heritage of western culture; yet a measure of firm belief is surely part of the good life. A free society means toleration, which in turn comes from openness of mind. But freedom also presupposes conviction; a free choice—unless it be wholly arbitrary (and then it would not be free)—comes from belief and ultimately from principle. A free society, then, cherishes both toleration and conviction. Yet the two seem incompatible. . . . How far should we go in the direction of the open mind?" (pp. 77–8). This is well said. But the Report does not reach a deeper source of inspiration, however, than the appreciation of responsibilities and benefits which belong to citizens "because they are Americans and are free" (p. xv). The weakness of the Report is the lack of clear and firm belief about the nature and destiny of man.*

In contrast with liberalism, totalitarianism is right in its insistence upon the need for a common faith, but wrong in seeking to establish faith by trampling on liberty, and shaping truth to political ends.†

There is only one possible solution of the contradiction between individual freedom and a common faith, and that is through a faith in which personal freedom is central, and the human soul of infinite value. Such a faith cannot impose itself

---

* The coy gymnastics of the following paragraph on religion deserve quotation. The italics are mine. *"We are not at all unmindful of the importance of religious belief in the completely good life.* But, given the American scene with its varieties of faith and even of unfaith, *we did not feel justified in proposing religious instruction as a part of the curriculum.* The love of God is tested by the love of neighbour; nevertheless the love of God transcends merely human obligations. *We must perforce speak in purely humanistic terms,* confining ourselves to the obligations of man to himself and to society. *But we have been careful so to delimit humanism as not to exclude the religious ideal.* Yet we are not arguing for an education which is student-centred. As man is the measure of the abstract values, so in their turn do these values measure man. Like an ellipse, an educational institution has two centres, not one. And although the geometrical metaphor forbids it, truth compels us to add a third, namely, society." (p. 76).

† Cf. the recent decree of the Council of the Academy of Sciences in Russia (26th August, 1948) which is aimed at the elimination of "bourgeois" biology and the establishment of Michurin biology with its doctrine that nurture prevails over nature. The doctrine provides a stimulus for the workers (i.e. directed effort can triumph over all obstacles) and has implications for man himself (i.e. man can be remade to fit the new social order). There is some irony in a sequence which begins by promising the remaking of the social order to fit the true needs of man and ends by promising the remaking of man to fit the social order. More recently, after a series of conferences of publishers, *Pravda* has announced that all publishing should submit to the "guidance and aid of local party organizations."

by authority without contradicting itself; it can promote unity of action only by appeal to responsible choice, and therefore depends for practical success upon goodwill. In the short run such a faith is at a manifest disadvantage as compared with an authoritarian creed that forces compliance. In the long run, however, the faith freely entered into is the stronger. But—and this is all-important—it will not survive at all in the conflict unless it has the power to suffer; and this means that there must be a full depth of conviction—conviction not only at the level of what we believe but at the level of why we believe it.

We are a long way from having such a faith at the back of our education. "Among all the responsibilities ignored or neglected since Rousseau, that of forming convictions is the most important."* If we are to educate people to be persons and not only technical and executive instruments, we must produce people not only who do their own thinking, but who do the kind of thinking that springs from deep convictions and also constantly illuminates those convictions. A system of education through which people can reach deep and strong convictions must itself spring from convictions about the nature and destiny of man. Such conviction implies a different philosophy from the relativism that prevails in the liberal west. John Dewey, for example, who may justly be regarded as the prophet and personal epitome of modern education, maintains that there is nothing to be said about the aim of education except that it is its own aim—a view which is the counterpart of Croce's view of history as having no purpose or value apart from the process itself.† The same relativism appears in Dewey's view that the needs of the individual have meaning only in relation to the needs of society, and *vice versa*. This view at least avoids the evils of thorough-going individualism and thorough-going collectivism. But it

---

* John F. Danby: "Literature and Dogma," *The Times Educational Supplement*, 30th October, 1948, p. 611.

† Dewey's insistence that education is its own aim was, of course, a necessary and timely protest against the view of education as a mere preparation for maturity, and Dewey deserves full credit for his vindication of childhood as having its own value and claims. But it is one thing to say that childhood has a meaning and value in itself, and another thing to say that there are no absolute standards of human life.

offers no escape from an endless reciprocal reference unless we can postulate some absolute good which determines the norm of both individual and society.

The writings of John Dewey illustrate not only the relativism of modern thinking, but also the modern tendency to pin faith to techniques because there is nothing else left to believe in. The following passage from Reinhold Niebuhr's *Gifford Lectures* is worth quoting at some length. "The fact that such a great proportion of modern thought since the eighteenth century preserves man's good opinion of himself in terms of a dubious naturalism which is not certain whether virtue is to be found in reason or in nature,* nor how the two are related to each other, is indicative of the degree to which modern man's easy conscience is derived from a false estimate of his transcendence over nature . . .

"Professor Dewey has a touching faith in the possibility of achieving the same results in the field of social relations which intelligence achieved in the mastery of nature. The fact that man constitutionally corrupts his purest visions of disinterested justice in his actual actions seems never to occur to him. Consequently he never wearies in looking for specific causes of interested rather than disinterested action. . . . The failure of the past and present are due to the fact that the scientific method 'has not been tried at any time with use of all the resources which scientific material and the experimental method now put at our disposal.' . . . As an educator, one of his favourite theories is that man's betrayal of his own ideals in action is due to faulty educational techniques which separate theory and practice, thought and action. . . .

"No one expresses modern man's uneasiness about his society

* To illustrate this point I cannot forbear quoting an incident that occurred recently at a meeting of a Board of Examiners, drafting examination papers for candidates seeking to qualify as teachers. A question on adolescence asked for a description of the conditions best conducive to "natural development." A member of the Board objected to this phrase and proposed the substitution of "right development," on the obvious grounds that "natural development" begged the question whether the natural was necessarily the right. The amendment met with a good deal of opposition from people who evidently found the phrase "right development" offensive as suggesting an old-fashioned authoritarian morality.

and complacency about himself more perfectly than John Dewey. One half of his philosophy is devoted to an emphasis upon what, in Christian theology, is called the creatureliness of man, his involvement in biological and social process. The other half seeks a secure place for disinterested intelligence above the flux of process, and finds it in 'organized co-operative inquiry'. Not a suspicion dawns upon Professor Dewey that no possible 'organized inquiry' can be as transcendent over the historical conflicts of interest as it ought to be to achieve the disinterested intelligence which he attributes to it. . . . There can be no 'free co-operative inquiry' which will not pretend to have achieved a more complete impartiality than is possible for human instruments of justice. . . . The solution at which Professor Dewey arrives is therefore an incredibly naïve answer to a much more ultimate and perplexing problem than he realizes."*

The weakness of our educational thinking is symptomatic of the weakness of our whole western culture. Just as our pre-industrial culture failed to assimilate the Industrial Revolution so—on a larger scale—the culture of the medieval west failed to assimilate the change that produced what we call the modern world—failed, that is, to maintain unity of thought and belief as against the centrifugal strains of the Renaissance and Reformation. Thus the modern world has no single, embracing view of life, but (comparably with the emergence of national, sovereign states) presents a number of separate, autonomous dominions of thought and knowledge.

The disintegration of the world-view is a reflection of the disintegration of the personal in modern society. Man the personal being is resolved into groups of factors, so that, for

---

* *The Nature and Destiny of Man,* Vol. I, pp. 117–119. In connection with Niebuhr's criticism, the following passage from Dewey's *Democracy and Education* (pp. 263–4) is interesting. "The problem of an educational use of science is then to create an intelligence pregnant with belief in the possibility of the direction of human affairs by itself. . . . Science represents the office of intelligence, in projection and control of new experiences, pursued systematically, intentionally, and on a scale due to freedom from limitations of habit. It is the sole instrumentality of conscious, as distinct from accidental, progress." The tendency among some psychologists to look to psychology as an instrument for reconstructing human nature and thus solving all human problems has been referred to elsewhere; see p. 21.

example, the modern novel gives us problems rather than people, functions rather than characters; or, again, man is resolved into types such as "the" worker, "the" bourgeois, "the" intellectual, and so on, "all classifiable in much the same way as insects,"* and presenting no significant variation within the type.

We can now see more clearly the essential nature of the modern world and its failure. The central meaning of the Renaissance was the liberation of the individual from the old authorities, intellectual, moral, and social. It was, in fact, the Discovery of Man. This affirmation of the new freedom was bound to make life at once immensely more interesting and immensely more difficult. The adventure could succeed only if man could synthesize the claims of individuality and society on the plane of the personal. There could be no return to the primitive, "natural" kind of collectivism of society before the emancipation of the individual; all the political and economic tensions of the modern world make that plain. A failure to achieve community at the personal level could only mean one of two things—anarchy, or a new, unnatural, pathological kind of collectivism. In either case the failure is a failure to achieve the truly personal, and its major symptom is therefore the depersonalization of life. That is why depersonalization is the great and disconcerting fact about modern civilization, and why the redemption of the personal is the supreme task of education.

If we turn from educational theory to educational practice we encounter the charge of unreality often brought against the modern curriculum. Too much of what is taught, whether for examinations or not, is of little help in understanding the world in which we live or as preparation for living in it. School and "life" are too far apart, and, what is worse, the gulf between them is accepted and taken for granted by the children, to whom it never occurs to seek any relation between school knowledge and life experience. In school, knowledge comes to us in "subjects"; in real life, experience does not come to us labelled "history,"

* Cf. George Orwell's review of Jean-Paul Sartre's *Portrait of an Anti-Semite* (*Observer*, 7th November, 1948). Orwell criticizes Sartre's "atomized vision of society" in which human beings disappear in types. N.B. How many educational writers are guilty of the monstrous abstraction "the child"?

"geography," or "chemistry," but in practical situations in which the historical, geographical, chemical, and many other aspects may be inextricably mixed up. For this reason we are not prepared to find our school knowledge helpful in the situations of real life. Not only so; much of what we are taught under the name of geography, history, or chemistry would never be of use to us, even if taught in a more usable way.

It would be unjust and misleading to speak of the unreality of educational content without also testifying to the increasing efforts that are being made, in matter and method, to remove this reproach. The educational literature of the last twenty years, in this country as well as in America, abounds in records of experiments in the reform of curriculum and method, designed to ensure that knowledge shall be relevant and usable. So great is the vogue for enlightenment that the words "activity" and "project" are beginning to have much the same effect on an average company of teachers as the word "veto" came to have on the Security Council.

The truth about the "unreality" of the curriculum might therefore seem to be, not that the curriculum is less related to the needs of life than it used to be, but that it is we who have become more aware of the right relations between learning and living and therefore more critical of the curriculum that falls short of the ideal.

In fact, both statements are true. The curriculum *has* drifted out of relation to needs. All educational content is originally useful. Latin was learnt because it was the *lingua franca* of Europe. Diplomatic and military history was learnt by the sons of the ruling class because it would help them to do their job. But Latin loses its usefulness when it ceases to be the language of learned discourse and public affairs, and new and dubious reasons for teaching it are invented. Diplomatic and military history is not edifying to the sons and daughters of artisans, who can benefit more from studying the history of the life and work of the people. Thus the traditional curriculum tends to become out of touch with social realities, by reason of the changes in the pattern of European culture and by reason of the extension of education to the mass of the people. Since the education of the people has been in the main a benefit dispensed from above, the subject-matter of it has been for the most part material originally designed for other purposes; the people have had the curriculum—or some of it—of the ruling class at secondhand, and educational reform has never caught up with educational need.

On the other hand, the political and economic changes of the last hundred years have made bare literacy quite inadequate as an equipment for the modern citizen. If it is true that universal education had to be undertaken because society had reached a stage of development at which it would no longer work unless people could read and write, it is no less true that we have now reached a stage of development at which our society will not work unless people can do a great deal more. We need not only a literate people but an educated people. It is our awareness of this need for an educated population that makes us more critical than we used to be of the content of education. So long as the aim of school instruction is no more than the Three R's, it is of relatively little importance whether or not the subject-matter helps us to understand the world we live in. But when the aim is to produce intelligent and responsible citizens, the content of education acquires a new importance.

The remoteness of much of our education from life is obviously connected with the failure of our culture to assimilate the Industrial Revolution. In particular this failure of assimilation has aggravated the cleavage between the "liberal" and "vocational" ideas in education. This cleavage, and its origin in the two main historical sources of our culture, will be more fully examined in a later chapter. For the moment it is enough to remind ourselves of the general acceptance by public opinion of two kinds of education, one of them described as "liberal" or "cultural," of no obvious practical use but carrying social prestige, and the other described as "technical" or "vocational," of immediate utility but without social prestige. The latter kind of education is valued because it has direct cash value, and the former because it has direct prestige value together with no little indirect cash value. This cleavage is a witness to our failure to achieve a unified culture, and is perhaps most apparent in our universities, not only in the caution with which the Faculties of Arts and Science regard one another, but, within the Faculty of Science, in a snobbish attitude of the "pure" scientist towards his "applied" colleague.*

The unreality of curriculum-content and the cleavage between the liberal and vocational traditions clearly weaken the effectiveness of education as a preparation for living. Moreover, the school as an institution stands apart from the rest of the community, with little overflow or penetration in either direction. The whole question of the relation between school and community is so important that a separate chapter is devoted to it. Furthermore, there is, in the internal government of many schools, insufficient practical education in citizenship through the exercise of freedom and responsibility. For example, in many grammar schools, the prefects appear to be little more than ushers, with such duties as the control of traffic in corridors, and with no share in the government of the school. †

Essential Elements in Modern Education

It has been the purpose of this chapter to discuss the special educational needs of our time and to suggest the kind of emphasis which education ought to have in order to meet those needs. It may be convenient to sum up the argument by stating what would appear to be the three essential elements of an education designed for the rescue of personal freedom in the modern world. The three elements correspond to the three great weaknesses that have been distinguished in modern education—its feeble grasp of ultimate values, its deficiency as an interpretation of the world we live in, and its inadequacy as a practical initiation into the life of society.

(i) One direct object of education must be an understanding

* "I'm a pure man, not an applied man," a physicist once said to me.
† During a good many years' experience of interviewing Sixth Form boys and girls for admission to Education Departments in universities, I have seldom received anything but a rather mystified negative to the question whether the prefects were consulted about the making or changing of school rules or on general questions of policy in the running of the school.

of the world in which we live. It is a good many years since the founders of the Association for Education in Citizenship said that, in the modern world, the adequate education of the citizen can no longer be taken for granted as a dependable by-product of "any good, general education." Not only are we now attempting the extremely difficult task of educating a whole population as responsible citizens, but the world in which their citizenship is to be exercised is a far more difficult world to understand even than the world of their grandfathers.

While it is clear that the business of explaining our world must be a positive educational responsibility and not something left to chance, this proposition should on no account be taken to mean that the material of study should be all, or even mostly, contemporaneous. The essential principle for the selection of material is relevance, not contemporaneity. The educational doctrine here advanced is not that every lesson should be a civics lesson, and every civics lesson consist of a visit to the gasworks, but rather that knowledge is dead unless it is instrumental in interpreting the world of active experience.* The history and literature of antiquity, for example, may be of supreme value in helping us to understand ourselves. Socrates and Isaiah may have messages for us more valuable than the deliverances of our contemporary oracles. Let the curriculum be as remote, in one sense, as we please, provided that it is contemporary in the other sense of laying hold on our world and interpreting it. To take a very simple example, the American High School pupils who addressed themselves to the question: Why was there no United States of Greece? were using their classical studies to illuminate their own world. By contrast, the wrong approach to classical studies is to say to one's pupils: "Learn this, but do not ask why. Be content that, by so doing, you will eventually become what is known as a well-educated person."

(ii) Even more important, perhaps, than the intellectual

* In support of this doctrine many telling words of Professor A. N. Whitehead's could be quoted, such as the following from *The Aim of Education and Other Essays.* "If education is not useful, what is it?" (p. 3). "Essentially culture should be for action." (p. 73). "The only use of a knowledge of the past is to equip us for the present." (p. 6).

attempt to understand the world we live in is direct experience of community living. Not only must the school afford opportunity within its own limits for learning how to live together—not only must the school seek to be a community in which true values prevail—but all elements in society must appreciate that they have an educational contribution to make. More will be said about this in the next chapter, the general thesis of which is that the expansion of the school into the outer world and the penetration of the outer world into the school are complementary processes, both of which are necessary to the achievement of reality and effectiveness in education. John Dewey was fond of the picture of the school as microcosm. But it is not enough for the school to seek to be a world. The world must also be a school. Education properly understood is an activity of the whole community. At the same time, the greatest contribution that the school can make towards the realization of this ideal of the educative society is the education of its members in the meaning of community. This the school can best do by striving to make the necessary personal relationships of school life (between the members of a form, between members of the staff, between teacher and class, and between prefects and other pupils) true examples of fellowship.

(iii) Thirdly, education should seek to reveal what has been called the "Vision of Greatness." We ought, that is to say, to help our pupils to enter, through literature and history, into their heritage of the best that has been thought and felt and done in the world. The vision alone is not enough. The world needs not only vision but faith. But faith cannot be manufactured. What we can do is to expose ourselves and our pupils to the great sources of inspiration, so that from the vision faith may grow.* A special plea may be made for more study of the Bible, not only because it is the source book of our religion and a very

---

* The attempt being made in some American universities to base a general education upon "the Great Books" is at least an experiment on the right lines. And to those (including a good many Americans) who sweep aside the great books with the comment: "A lot of things have happened since they were written," one is tempted to retort: "I hope a lot more will happen before they are forgotten."

important element in our cultural tradition, but also because people among whom the Bible is studied and known are bound to be immeasurably enriched, and people who forget the Bible are bound to be immeasurably impoverished, in their understanding of the human heart and mind.

An important part of the Vision is the contemplation of great persons and through them the better understanding of the meaning of the personal in human life. We must show the personal in its relation to technics and the mass. A community can lose personal quality even as an accumulator can run down. And personal quality can degenerate in two directions—towards animalism and towards mechanism. Both forms of degeneration are displayed by the mass in a technological age. In this age the mass assumes a new and dangerous role. No longer is the mass inert, more or less independent of the aristocratic culture developed among the educated few. The mass to-day is educated enough—active enough—to be easily manipulated by means of the new and powerful techniques for influencing opinion. And, in accepting manipulation, the mass extorts its conditions, which are a lowering of all standards to the level of what the mass likes and can understand. The mass is at once the sacrificial victim and the god to whom the sacrifice is offered. The exploitation of the mass is also the uprising of the mass against the aristocratic in culture—demanding that everything, including learning, shall be used for the service of the mass, and that the standards of the mass shall be the universal criteria. Quantity triumphs over quality. The mass, by its own limitations, determines what shall be accepted in art, literature, religion.*

As against this degeneration of values, we must set the personal as the embodiment and guarantee of the true aristocratic principle. The true aristocrat in any age and in any country is he whose behaviour is most fully personal. The authority for what he does is his own, not derived; he identifies himself with his actions, takes full responsibility for their consequences, and, so

---

* One has only to look at the lengths to which popularization has gone in America, and the efforts which the attempt to maintain cultural standards is costing those in America who are fighting for intellectual quality, to realize that this description is not merely a flight of lurid imagination.

to speak, authenticates them. Historically, social aristocracies have always possessed in fair measure this quality, which is the valid ground of the respect in which they have been held.

There is another aspect of the Vision of Greatness which is worth noticing. It is probable that right thinking is connected with right feeling even more closely than we realize, and that the Vision of Greatness can release intellectual as well as emotional forces. That is to say, behaviour which is influenced by the right values will tend to be not only nobler but more intelligent. If that is so, the problem of how to educate a people to be capable of intelligent and responsible behaviour is not solely a question of Intelligence Quotients. In that case, the prospect for democracy is brighter than it would otherwise be.

Additional Note I
Voluntary Service

The passage in this chapter which advocates the more extensive seeking of vocation in voluntary service had been written before I read Lord Beveridge's *Voluntary Action* (Allen & Unwin, 1948). The following suggestions in Lord Beveridge's book are important in this connection—

(1) The principle of the contributory hospital scheme should be applied to wider purposes, such as the establishment of welfare funds to meet a variety of needs—the care of the aged and of children, holiday schemes, etc.

(2) It should be possible for citizens to register in local organizations for voluntary action. Such registration might be done through Citizens' Advice Bureaux.

(3) The State should finance more extensively the training of staff for different kinds of voluntary service. "When charity meant giving money or food or coals it needed little training. When voluntary service means running a Citizens' Advice Bureau or a Training College for the Disabled, the best intentions are not enough without skill." (p. 314.) Reference is made to Miss Younghusband's *Report on the Employment and Training of Social Workers* (Carnegie Trust, 1947).

(4) An independent corporation, endowed by the State, should be established, alongside such corporations as the Carnegie and Pilgrim Trusts, to promote social advance by voluntary action.

(5) The Friendly Societies should be encouraged "to lift their sights and enlarge their scope beyond monetary insurance to provision of services and neighbourly mutual aid." (p. 309.)

Lord Beveridge's general view of the place of voluntary action in the community is expressed in the following passages—

"Voluntary Action is needed to do things which the State should not do in the giving of advice, or in organizing the use of leisure. It is needed to get services rendered which cannot be got by paying for them." (p. 301, 2.)

"The State should encourage Voluntary Action of all kinds for social advance. . . . It should in every field of its growing activity use where it can, without destroying their freedom and their spirit, the voluntary agencies for social advance, both of social conscience and of philanthropy. This is one of the marks of a free society." (p. 318.)

The solution of the problem of freedom in the planned society would seem to lie in the promotion of voluntary activity, not in competition with, but within systems of public administration. It is not inevitable that public administration should be oppressive and impersonal. A headmaster of a fully maintained grammar school recently said to me: "Except for the fact that our money is provided for us, we might be an independent school."

Additional Note II
The Emergence of the Individual and Its Importance in Social Development

It may be convenient to summarize the analysis of social development which has been suggested in the first section of Chapter IV and in other parts of this book.

Stage I. The pre-individualistic stage. A world of *"status"* (Cf. Sir H. Maine), in which the masses were more or less inert (the primitive collective), and the active minority was still largely bound by custom.

Stage II. The change (in Maine's phrase) *"from status to contract"* through the assertion of the individual (in the Renaissance) who, emancipated from the old authorities, was now at liberty to pursue, not only truth and beauty where he found them, but wealth in open competition.

Stage III. The modern dilemma. The emergence of the free individual greatly increased the tension between individual and society and made the resolution of that tension much more difficult than before, since it can no longer be resolved at the level of more or less unconscious habit. We can never go back to the primitive collective, and the new collective is different.

The tension between individual and society was increased because the assertion of the individual meant—

(i) theoretical, political equality, since all human beings have equal rights as such.

(ii) practical, economic inequality, owing to free competition.

Modern man tends to escape from the tension in one of two directions—

(i) By denial of social responsibility. The anarchy of individualism.

(ii) By sacrificing liberty for security. The new collective, into which man tends to plunge, differs from the original primitive collective because it means the denial and suppression of individual values which have been acknowledged and experienced. It thus bears a somewhat similar relation to the primitive collective as "sin" bears to primal innocence.

Dangerous as such analogies are, it is tempting to compare these extremes of social development with the psychological patterns of manic-depressive insanity and dementia praecox. The one is the extreme of extroversion, impulsive and unselfcritical, subject to alternating booms and slumps of enthusiasm and depression. The other is the extreme of introversion, full of intense but mysterious activity behind a curtain, and meeting the outer world either with an uncompromising "no" or with a stream of paranoiac fantasia.

Meanwhile the ideal solution is quite obvious, namely the community of free fellowship. The practical business of democracy is to combine liberty and order in such a way as to foster the development of the community of freedom and responsibility. The national tradition of our own country is such that Britain has a special opportunity and obligation to demonstrate to the rest of the world an approximation to this essential democracy. In such an enterprise, education must be of first-rate importance.

V
School and Community

REFERENCE has been made to the unreality of a good deal of our educational content, and to the isolation, and insulation, of the school in relation to the rest of the community. The view was put forward that education can only be what it ought to be in proportion as it becomes an activity of the whole community.

The School an Artificial Device

There has always been education but there have not always been schools. In Shakespeare's time few people in England went to school or learnt to read and write. But this lack of literacy does not mean that people were uneducated. In some ways they were better educated than their representatives to-day. The peasant in the village learnt the arts and skills of farming, together with much traditional wisdom about earth and sky and living things. In the town the boy was apprenticed to a master craftsman in whose household he lived with other apprentices, and where he learnt not only a trade but the ways of business and the rules and customs of the Guilds, and gained experience of varied human nature. For the girl, the home with its still-room, loom, and herb garden offered a better domestic education than it does in these days of canned food, ready-made clothes, and queueing. The whole people shared a true, indigenous, popular culture with a rich heritage of customs, tales, games, and music. And the Church provided, not only sound moral instruction and a framework of social life, but that "solemn bass of mystery and the unseen" to which "each man plays his own descant."*

Schools and universities were, nevertheless, a very important part of Elizabethan England, though few attended them. In the primitive community, however, there is no need for schools at

* *John Inglesant*, Ch. XXIII (Cardinal Rinuccini speaking).

all. In the African tribe the young people can learn all they need (or could do so before the coming of the European trader) by simply growing up in the tribal community. In fact the life of the tribe, with its daily and seasonal tasks, its initiation ceremonies and other rituals, *is* the school.

At a certain stage in the development of civilization schools become necessary. But the school is inevitably an artifice, separated from the rest of the life of the community. From the first establishment of special institutions for conducting education, and of a special class of professional teachers, education becomes artificial and a divorce occurs between school and life. The establishment of the first schools thus lays upon the future an unending task of re-integrating education with the life of the community.

Realistic Curriculum

If the purpose of education is purely academic, a divorce between school and life need not be a source of great uneasiness. Instruction in the Three R's, or, at a higher level, advanced scholarship in classical languages or mathematics, or even pure science, needs little or no contact with "life." It is possible, under certain conditions, for a culture to endure for centuries in which the material of education has nothing to do with the business of life. Thus in China public officials were required to pass a test in archery long after firearms had become the established means of warfare. "China's pursuit of educational aims regardless of their congruity with the circumstances of life led in the long run to considering education, not as a preparation for participation in adult activities, but as an end in itself. Indeed, for centuries the ideally-educated man in China was the scholar. To be sure, the scholar was also the civil servant, but nevertheless in later centuries much if not most of what he had to learn was quite unrelated to civil affairs."* Even the value of the content of the classical literature was largely lost owing to the habit of memorizing by rote, which tended to destroy meaning; though it should be remembered that Confucius himself uttered a warning

* J. S. Brubacher: *A History of the Problems of Education*, p. 2.

against this very thing: "Learning without thought is labour lost."*

The separation of the school from life, and the unreality of curriculum, become matters of grave concern when education undertakes the responsibility of explaining the world in which we live. It then becomes necessary to bring the world into the school and the school out into the world. A century ago the aim of elementary education in this country was to produce a literate people. To-day literacy is not enough, and it is clear that democracy cannot hope to work without an educated people—educated, that is, in the sense of being capable of intelligent and responsible behaviour.

During the present century, as we have become increasingly aware that much of the traditional curriculum is academic and much of the knowledge taught not usable,† efforts have been made to relate the work of the school more directly with the life of the world outside. More realistic methods of teaching have been evolved (e.g. the revolution in the teaching of languages); and functional rather than formal ways of organizing subject-matter have been found (e.g. the "project").

Behind all modern experiments in the reform of the curriculum is the principle that education should be grounded in the genuine concerns of the pupil, and should help him, by means of material and activities appropriate to his present stage of development, to get his bearings in his world. No experiment perhaps is more characteristic of the modern trend than the American Eight-Year Study,‡ the general purpose of which was to establish a relationship between High School and College that would permit and encourage the reform of curriculum in the secondary school. The experiment was in progress from 1933 to 1941. Thirty schools took part, experimenting in various ways with more free curricula, and nearly three hundred receiving colleges and

---

* *Ibid.*, pp. 166–7.

† For the reasons for this increasingly critical attitude towards educational content, see pp. 66–69.

‡ See the five-volume report entitled: *Adventure in American Education* (Harper, 1942). Vol. I, *The Story of the Eight-Year Study*, gives a general survey of the whole work. See also Thayer, Zachry, and Kotinsky: *Reorganizing Secondary Education* (Appleton-Century, 1939).

universities agreed to suspend normal matriculation tests to set the schools free to experiment. The aims of the curricula were—

(i) to meet genuine student concerns (e.g. How can I prepare for a job? How can I make and keep friends, or improve my relations with parents, brothers and sisters? Why do I think and feel as I do? Am I normal? What can I believe in?) and

(ii) to interpret the American view of life.

There is a certain naïveté about the whole of this experiment; but it is also refreshingly adventurous. In the work of the schools book-study was increasingly supplemented by neighbourhood study, teacher-pupil planning groups were formed, and conferences of teachers, parents, and pupils were held. The attempt to help pupils to a better understanding of themselves and their world was made in some cases by giving considerably more time to the direct study of contemporary affairs and the neighbourhood and in others by the more conservative methods of seeking the relevant implications of the conventional studies. Whatever method was used, there seems little doubt that studies became more alive and realistic and that pupils were more disposed to work from interest in what they were doing.

The results were tested by the study of nearly 1500 matched pairs of students—one of each pair from a participating school and the other from elsewhere, but as alike as possible in other respects such as intelligence and social background. The students from the Thirty Schools turned out to be slightly better in university studies as judged by the ordinary college standards, and were assessed as superior in intellectual curiosity, clear thinking, resourcefulness, interest in current affairs, and participation in general activities and the holding of responsible positions. Appropriately one of the schools' conclusions about curriculum is that inert subject-matter should give place to content that is alive and pertinent to the problems of youth and modern civilization.*

* While there is an important sense in which this conclusion is true—and no one would have endorsed it more whole-heartedly than Professor A. N. Whitehead—it is also important to repeat emphatically that the relevant is not necessarily the contemporaneous. There is a regrettable tendency in some quarters to make light of the cultural contribution of the past.

The connection between the school and the life of the rest of the community is never so convincing as when work done in the school is of direct value to the community. In manual activities it is fairly easy for pupils to contribute usefully to the community (e.g. by repairing machinery),* and wartime short- ages gave a stimulus to experiments in this field. † In other school activities it is less easy to find work that is of practical value, but it is very important to seek opportunities of doing so. Suggestive examples are: the assistance given by pupils of grammar schools in the recent land utilization surveys and, in one area, in the preparation of the Ministry of Education's *Visual Unit* on local surveys;‡ contributions by groups of boys and girls to books and other publications;§ and the use of work done by one group of children as teaching material with other groups.‖

It is difficult to exaggerate the value of this kind of reality in education. There is all the difference in the world between something done merely as an academic exercise and something done for a practical purpose, just as there is a world of difference between a question asked in order to find out whether the victim of interrogation knows the correct answer, and a question asked in order that the information given in reply may be of interest and value to others. Half the frustration and futility of education is due to the fact that the minds of pupils and teachers alike are

* For many years the workshops at Oundle School have repaired farming machinery. Alternatively, the school workshops can produce materials for the school itself. I recall a Home Office school for delinquent boys where the brickyard not only produced the bricks for building an extension to the school but also provided a first-rate education in close co-operation.

† E.g. the making of toys for public nurseries.

‡ Ministry of Education: *Visual Unit; Social Studies*, 1948, Pamphlet No. 10. See also Helen Merrell Lynd: *Field Work in College Education* (Columbia Uni- versity Press, 1945). An account of surveys which the Sarah Lawrence College was asked to undertake (e.g. for the Yonkers Family Welfare Society) and courses which the college was asked to provide for the general public (e.g. on nutrition).

§ E.g. the section contributed by Gower Street Senior Boys' School, Aston, to *Our Birmingham* (1943), the first of a series of publications by Messrs. Cadbury, of which others are *Changing Britain*, Nos. 1, 2, and 3. *Our Birmingham* (1s.), and the other Cadbury publications, are obtainable from the University of London Press.

‖ The use of the work of one class as material for teaching other classes is described by Mr. A. T. Glover in his *New Teaching for a New Age* (Nelson, 1946).

enslaved by the convention that school activities are only exercises and classroom questions only tests. The children themselves are so dominated by this idea that it is often only with the greatest difficulty that one can convince them that one really wants their opinion, whatever it may be, and not "the right answer." One of the high spots in the teaching career of one of my colleagues was the moment when, after prolonged and tactful efforts on her part to penetrate into the region of genuine feelings, one small person wonderingly asked: "Oh Miss, do you *want* what we think?" The point is well made in the following passage from a recent book on the technique of study: "Part of the difficulty of writing formal exercises arises from the fact that there is no real reader to write for. Matters are not much better when the prospective reader is an examiner. The reason is the same in both cases—there is no real communication."* What is literally true of the written composition is true in a more general way of all school work which is done without hope of its being of interest or value to other people.

Education as the Community in Action

Even more important than the participation of the school in the life of the community is the participation of the community in education. It is not too much to say that education can never be fully and properly related to the life of the community—the school can never do its job—until the whole community takes its share in the work of education. By that means alone can education recover, in the context of civilized society, something of the primitive naturalness of growing up in the life of the community.

Without any detraction from the value of John Dewey's

* Neil Wright: *Teach Yourself to Study* (U.T.P., 1945), p. 221. See also the Report of the Hartog Committee on *The Marking of English Essays* (International Institute Examinations Enquiry, Macmillan, 1941). The report contains the recommendation (p. 142) that "the practice of asking pupils from the age of 13 and upwards to write 'compositions' termed 'essays' be abandoned; and that they be asked instead to write compositions on subjects about which they may reasonably be expected to have a fund of ideas and a sufficient knowledge which they could express *for a given audience and with a given object in view*; and that before the writing is actually begun the audience and the object be either defined by the teacher or the examiner concerned, or left to the pupil himself to determine." (Italics are mine.)

contribution to educational practice, it may be questioned whether the idea of the school as microcosm—i.e. as an image of the world—offers the best approach to the problem of reality in education. The all-important thing about the school is, not that it should present an image of the world, but that it should be in actual connection with the world at as many points as possible. To put it differently, the school that is insulated from the world cannot faithfully present an image of the world, and therefore cannot satisfy Dewey's requirements. Dewey himself appreciates this, of course; but interpretations of Dewey's thought at second-hand have sometimes given a misleading impression.

The enormous extension of the social services in recent years has had two very important effects. It has expanded our idea of what education means, so that we are now prepared to think of vocational guidance, child care, the Youth Service, as belonging to "education" no less than school instruction. It has also spread the responsibility for educational activities more widely over the community, so that more agencies and more kinds of people are involved in work that is essentially educational.

But this engagement of society at large in the work of education must go farther still, and we ought to make some effort to see what the ideal of education as the whole community in action would mean. Vocational guidance (involving representatives of industry) would have to extend into an Educational Advice Service.* Public services, such as the Post Office, would have (as some of them do now) to co-operate with the schools in showing boys and girls how these services work. Industries would have to co-operate with the schools in showing boys and girls what types of employment they offer and so help school-leavers to choose their jobs. Industries and public services would have to develop very considerably their "public relations" departments, so that the education of the public as intelligent users or consumers would be as integral a part of their business as the production of commodities or the provision of facilities.

* See the suggestion for Educational Advice Bureaux in F. M. Earle: *Reconstruction in the Secondary School.*

There would have to be a great expansion in the field of further and adult education, and the artificial cleavage between instruction and recreation would have to be overcome in the field of leisure-time education. In particular a new accent would be laid upon education for marriage and family relationships. In the centre of the picture is the educational responsibility of the home. The home where worth-while books are never read, where parents are constantly out in the evenings, where dubious moral standards are accepted, and where conversation never rises above triviality, is not the kind of home that helps the school to do its work. Nor can the school bear the whole burden. The mother who replied to a criticism of her small child's bad behaviour: "Oh, I know I can't do anything with her. But I don't care. You see, she starts school next week" was making an unfair demand of the school. Parents must be partners with the school, and everything possible should be done to help them to appreciate the need for their contribution to this partnership, so that school and home can deal together with problems arising either at school or at home.*

The full participation of the community in education would mean the emergence, both in idea and in actual organization, of a fuller interpretation of the meaning of education, at present no more than adumbrated by the multiplicity of separate and imperfectly co-ordinated services, medical, educational, disciplinary, recreational, and so on. The absorption of education, in the narrower sense, into such a comprehensive service, and the consequent enlargement of what education means, may be far more important than any changes in the schools themselves, and may constitute the real educational revolution of our time. This revolution would imply nothing less than the acceptance of the priority of educational values throughout the community —that is to say, the belief that the purpose of society is the good life and not something else such as wealth or power. It means,

* Is Mary backward in her school work? What light can her parents throw on the possible causes? Is she going to bed too late? Is she doing too many domestic chores? If John's mother finds him difficult to manage at home, what help can she get by talking it over with John's teacher? Perhaps John's father is away from home. If so, what has that to do with it, and what can be done to give the boy the right sort of leisure interests instead of running wild with undesirable companions?

in other words, a kind of society different from that which exists, and in which people are treated as ends in themselves—in which, for example, the boy or girl who goes into paid employment on leaving school must be regarded as a ward of the community at least until the age of eighteen, and young people's paid occupations should be considered from the point of view of their educative value to the young people themselves rather than from the point of view of their contribution to national production.

The approach towards a kind of society whose purpose is the good life and in which all members are treated as ends can only be gradual, and there are certain pre-requisites for any substantial advance in that direction, of which perhaps the chief are: a certain basic economic security, a reasonable measure of international security, and a common belief in certain moral and spiritual values.

Remote though the ideal may be, it is salutary to see what its practical implications are. Nor should we fail to welcome signs of progress and to press every advantage. Consciousness of present shortcomings often blinds us to what has in fact been achieved, not least in education. Industry to-day, for example, is much more favourably disposed towards education than it was a quarter of a century ago, and many employers are anxious to extend the educational facilities available to their employees. It is true that business firms have initiated educational schemes from motives that are not purely educational. But it is far better that education should be promoted than not promoted; and in any case it would be unrealistic to expect a business firm to undertake something that would not pay. The fact that it pays does not make it bad education.

As Plato was well aware, education cannot be what it ought to be except in a perfect society, and yet the perfect society can be created, if at all, only by education. There may be no theoretical escape from this dilemma. But in practical life it is often possible to break into a vicious circle which is logically impregnable. An actual society can be changed, little by little, in the direction of the ideal community by the leaven within it of spontaneous fellowships of different kinds. What is more, this is the only way in which the quality of a whole society can be improved. Changes in political and economic systems are negative measures in that they can do no more than create opportunity. Government cannot create virtue any more than it can create freedom. The real quality of any society depends on the estimate at which personal values are held, and this in turn depends on the effective demonstration of the meaning of true community through free fellowship.

In this connection it is worth recalling something that was said in a previous chapter—that the most important contribution which the school can make to the realization of the ideal of the educative society is the practical education of its members in the meaning of community. The school can do nothing better for the education of citizens than to make its boys and girls members of a true community in which are combined liberty and order, freedom and responsibility; in which human personality is respected for its own sake, regardless of age or other irrelevant circumstance; which recognizes the authority of reason and experience, not of fear and status; and where liberty of thought has its complement in the responsibility for making one's own choice of opinions, and love rather than neutrality is the guarantee of intellectual freedom.

If the school's supreme function is practical education in fellowship, some attention ought to be given to the conditions that have to be fulfilled in order that the school can perform that function. Obviously the most important conditions are the personal qualities of the teachers and their beliefs, and there can be no remedy for inadequacy at this level. But there are a good many other things which are within the control of administration and which can greatly help or hinder the creation of moral and spiritual values. We should be prepared to review, from the point of view of their bearing on the creation of community, such things as school government, size of classes, the relation of curriculum and methods to pupils' real needs and interests, and the use of modern knowledge in the handling of individual cases of backwardness or maladjustment.

VI

The Sources of Our Educational Tradition

"THE mythical figure of Plato," wrote Dr. A. N. Whitehead, "may stand for modern liberal education as does that of St. Benedict for technical education."* It is the purpose of this chapter to examine the historical sources of our western culture, and therefore of our educational tradition. Two sources have to be distinguished, the Hellenic and the Hebrew-Christian (or Classical and Biblical), and the essential differences between them considered. It must also be observed that these two main traditions have certain values in common which are seriously threatened in our own day, partly by a sceptical "failure of nerve" (in the phrase which J. B. Bury used of the declining morale of the Græco-Roman world) and partly by positive antagonistic forces. An attempt at a final analysis of these factors in relation to one another belongs rather to Part II of this book. This chapter is concerned only with the two sources of western culture. A preliminary examination of the liberal and vocational ideas in education affords a convenient approach to the underlying problems of the relation between thought and action and of the nature of Reality, on which the cleavage between the Hellenic and Hebrew-Christian traditions occurs.

The Liberal and Vocational Ideas in Education

We are familiar with two points of view on the aims of education, identifying themselves with the "liberal" and "vocational" principles, and usually suspicious of one another.† On the one hand is the ideal of the well-stocked, well cultivated mind, the gracious and well-disciplined character. In this view knowledge,

---

* *The Aims of Education and Other Essays*, p. 70.
† See page 68 for a previous reference to the cleavage between the "liberal" and "vocational," or "cultural" and "technical" ideas.

learning, personal development are good in themselves, and the nobility of the educational process ought not to be degraded, nor its full reach short-circuited, by the subordination of ultimate aims to immediate utilities. The highest purpose of education is to produce good men, and the production of good tradesmen, and even of good citizens, is an inferior operation which must not be allowed to interfere with the other. This notion of liberal education* derives ultimately from Aristotle, and owes its name to his view of the proper education for free men—men of affairs who had no need to concern themselves with mechanical and menial tasks. In a famous passage he distinguishes between "the liberal arts, fit for free men and conducive to the exercise of virtue" and the "illiberal," banausic occupations which "deform the body and degrade the soul." (*Politics*, VIII. 2.) This view stands in marked contrast to that of the Hebrew teacher and high court judge, Hillel of Jerusalem: "Let no man say: 'I am a priest' or 'I am a learned man', for a man should rather flay a carcase in the street than cease to earn his bread with his hands."†

The traditional notion of "liberal culture," ill-defined as it is, has two features that belong to its origin—the disparagement of manual labour and the assumption of a social élite. In our own day, the anti-manual prejudice has become an anti-vocational prejudice, and the social élite is more and more becoming an intellectual élite. But the fundamental distinction remains between a kind of education that is prestigious and one that is merely useful. At its best the liberal ideal has affirmed the full and balanced development of personality and, to use a phrase of Whitehead's, the redemption of "labour from the associations of aimless toil." At its worst it has provided a dignified camouflage for a good deal of scholastic humbug.

In antithesis to the liberal ideal stands the view that all education is in the broad sense vocational—that people cannot be educated

---

* The reader will inevitably think of J. H. Newman in this connection. As an illustration of the rashness of all generalization—of which this chapter almost entirely consists—it is well to' remember that Newman advocated the establishment of a university department of brewing.

† Quoted by Robert Graves in a letter to *The Times*, 2nd March, 1946.

in perfectly general terms, but only in relation to some particular kind of society and some particular function in that society, that a culture which is out of touch with the life and work of the people is dead and that vocational bias does not degrade education but gives it significance and that there is in fact no meaning or purpose in developing personal qualities and abilities unless they are used in the service of the community. A system of education conceived on these lines will aim primarily at enabling the pupils to understand the world they are living in and to prepare themselves for living usefully and happily in it. At its worst vocational education is the acquisition of mere tricks of the trade. At its best it is the consecration of service, and can be as generous and philosophical as the apostles of the liberal tradition could wish, while possessing the added urgency of meaning that comes from direct reference to social utility.*

We know these two standpoints, and we know that the anti-thesis between them is a false one—that a true education cannot consist of studies and activities that are *merely* "cultural" or *merely* "useful," that in actual fact all really good education transcends the antithesis. And we can recognize the truth and value of each side of the antithesis. The value of the liberal tradition lies in its affirmation that man is more than his techniques and life more than a complex of economic processes, and that a man is liberalized by his occupation in proportion as he effectively grasps its humane implications and lives in the light of a philosophy evolved from those implications. The value of the vocational principle is its assertion that a man's duty to his fellows has first claim on him, that the satisfaction of fully developed faculties ought not to be an end in itself but a by-product of a useful life, and that an idea has to become incarnate in action at a specific time and place before it can avail anything.

It may be observed that the popular notion of liberal education

* It would be unjust to Aristotle to suggest that he did not see the service of the community as the aim of education. In fact, from one point of view he subjected the individual too much to the needs of the State. It could, in fact, be truly said that, for Aristotle, liberal education was essentially vocational. Nevertheless it is among the Greeks that the historical origins of the "liberal" tradition, with its defects as well as its virtues, must be sought.

overlooks the important fact (of which, incidentally, the Greeks were well aware) that *all* education has originally been vocational, in the sense of equipping particular kinds of people for known functions in a specific society. The apparent dilettantism of the classical education of an eighteenth-century gentleman conceals what was in fact the vocational training of a ruling class in the age of the amateur. It was, all things considered, a very efficient instrument for its purpose. Our trouble to-day is that we no longer live in the age of the amateur but in the age of the technician, and we have never evolved an education for technicians which is, in the true sense of the word, liberal. As a matter of fact the modern exponents of liberal education are themselves more and more becoming technicians. A professor of Classics, or of English Literature, is doing a highly technical job, for which he has received a special vocational training. That is the proper light in which to regard his work, and we shall thereby be reminded that the liberality of education is not determined by its content—there is no sense in saying that Greek is "liberal" and engineering is not. What is less proper is to inflict the same kind of training as the professor received, or a diluted form of it, upon young students most of whom have no intention or prospect of becoming professors, and withal to do so in the name of liberal education.

Philosophical Presuppositions of the Liberal and Vocational Traditions

Here, then, are two contrasted educational traditions, the one making the fully developed mind and character an end in itself, and historically associated with a social or intellectual élite, and the other making usefulness the primary aim (of which personal fulfilment should be a by-product) and historically associated with the essential labour of the community; the one nurtured in the universities and grammar schools and tending to formality of content and method, the other more functional in approach and transmitted through the guilds to our own works schools, technical schools and colleges, and the Faculties of Applied Science in the universities. Any attempt to distinguish the two traditions in this way is, of course, misleading, since the traditions are far more mixed up together than such an over-simplification would suggest.

It is not the purpose of this chapter, however, to discuss contemporary types of education, but to examine underlying principles. It will be clear from what has already been said that a good deal more is involved than the familiar issue between "liberal" and "vocational" education. This issue is in fact part of the larger problem of the relation of Θεωρία and πρᾶξις, thought and life, the spirit and the flesh—the problem, in fact, of the nature of Truth and Reality.

It is an over-simplification, but a legitimate and useful one, to say that the texture of western thought is woven of two fundamental interpretations of man (one Classical and one Biblical) and of two corresponding views of the nature of Truth and Reality. Socrates believed that perfection, or "wisdom," was attainable by human reason if the soul could free itself, by discipline or death, from the bonds of the flesh. Truth belonged to the realm of the changeless and the unseen, and was not to be found in the flux of history. To the Hebrew prophets, or to St. Paul, man is not self perfectible, for the conflict in man is not between his higher and lower natures, but proceeds from a contradiction within the highest part of man, and is manifested as "sin" which is the revolt of the divine in man against his creatureliness, making him desire to be free *from* God instead of free *for* God.* From this frustration man needs redemption by the grace of God. To save, God enters the world—enters history —and Truth is to be found, not in abstracted contemplation, but in the turmoil of historical and personal experience. Truth is something that has to be lived, not merely beheld.

For the purpose of the present inquiry, the Classical and Biblical doctrines of man are of more interest than the respective beliefs about ultimate reality. But, since the former are more readily intelligible in the context of the latter, it is worth while

---

* See pp. 22-23, where the "sense of sin" is defined as the healthy recognition of the conflict in man as a creature at odds with himself and needing at-one-ment. The whole of Chapter II is relevant in this connection.

to summarize the main lines of Greek and Hebrew thought about the nature of reality and its relation to the world of forthcoming experience. Brief as this summary must be, it is important to acknowledge the variety of opinions among the Greeks, and to reckon with it in making any generalizations. The opposite extremes are represented by Heraclitus, for whom there was no abiding reality but only perpetual flux (whence it would appear doubtful whether any true knowledge is possible), and Parmenides, for whom everything was illusion except the one ultimate and unchanging reality.

It was in protest against the Heraclitean doctrine of flux that Socrates propounded his theory of the existence of permanent natures ("forms" or "Ideas") beyond the world of sensible things, and not knowable by the senses. Plato made Socrates' eternal natures the foundation of his philosophy. His doctrine of the soul, as the link between the eternal and unchanging world of Ideas and the world of ever-changing phenomena, did something to bring the two worlds into relation with each other, as also did his theory of knowledge, by which learning consists of the resuscitation, under the influence of education, of these dim recollections of the perfect Ideas which the soul brings with it into this world. But Plato adhered to the view that the highest kind of knowledge is not received through the senses, that the body is a handicap to the mind, that in the perfect society the philosopher would rule, and that the highest life is the contemplative life.

Aristotle went farther than Plato in imagining a relationship between the world of Ideas and the world of phenomena. In his view the Idea, or universal, is not to be thought of as existing separately but is always found in connection with the particular instances of its manifestation. There is a continuous process by which matter, by being invested with its appropriate forms, becomes what it should become. Everything thus tends towards perfection, and everything is best understood in terms of what it is capable of becoming. In line with his metaphysic was Aristotle's doctrine of learning by which sensory experience, so far from being despised, was held essential, since the intellect could not initiate. As the later schoolmen put it: *"Nihil in intellectu quod non prius in sensu."* Nevertheless, although Aristotle had moved a long way from Plato, he still maintained the primacy of the intellect and held that the highest activity was contemplative. "The activity of God must be contemplative, and of human activities, therefore, that which is most akin to this must be most of the nature of happiness." (*Ethics*, x. 8.)

The Neoplatonists, through their doctrine of mediators, and in the mystical notion of identification with God in ecstasy (Plotinus), made their own contribution to the problem of relating the world of eternity and the world of time. But, notwithstanding the susceptibility of Christianity to the influence of Neoplatonism, the effect of the Neoplatonic doctrine of mediators was to keep the two worlds apart rather than reconcile them, and the mystical union, whatever else it might signify, means the loss of personality and therefore of personal relationship.

It is in their failure to conceive of the relation between man and the Universe as a personal one, in which Reality, or God, is ever active and concerned about the life of man, that all the Greek thinkers can be grouped together. Even Stoicism, which became a religion and believed in the all-pervading providence of God and the duty of man devoutly to acquiesce, did not conceive of God as being particularly interested in man. For the Stoics there was no divine love and no divine grace. "Theirs not to reason why."

In strong contrast to the Greek notion of a changeless, tranquil Reality beyond time and space, and of contemplation as the highest good, Hebrew thought started with an ever-active God, Who did not disdain to use His hands, Who worked and expected man to work also. The God of the Hebrews was personally concerned about man, and His love for man, revealed throughout the Old Testament, was fulfilled in Christ.

The theme of God active in history runs right through the Biblical literature. At the beginning, God works. "God created . . . and saw that it was good" (Gen. i. 1, 10). God commands. "God spake these words and said . . ." (Exod. xx. 1). God leads His people. "The Lord thy God is with thee whithersoever thou goest" (Joshua i. 9). The Psalmist, whether he laments: "My God, my God, why hast Thou forsaken me?" (Ps. xxii. 1) or sings: "The Lord is my shepherd; I shall not want," (Ps. xxiii. 1), never doubts the personal nature of the relationship. "Unto Thee, O Lord, will I call" (Ps. xxviii. 1). The prophets proclaim God's word about righteousness. "I hate, I despise your feasts; neither will I regard the peace offerings of your fat beasts. But let judgment roll down like waters and righteousness as a mighty stream" (Amos v. 22, 24). And they appeal to the course of history for evidence of God's purpose, as in Isaiah's great treatise on foreign politics. "Your country is desolate; your cities are burnt with fire. . . . Therefore saith the Lord . . ." (Is. i. 7, 24). From the depths of the experience of the Exile rises the vision of the chosen servant of God, redeeming through suffering. "Comfort ye, My people. . . Behold My servant whom I uphold, in whom My soul delighteth. I have put my spirit upon him. . . . He was wounded for our transgressions. . . . He was oppressed, yet he humbled himself. . . . The Spirit of the Lord is upon me . . . that He might be glorified." (Is. xl. 1, xlii. 1, liii. 5, 7, lxi. 1, 3.) Finally the eternal Logos "through Whom the world was made" but "Whom the world knew not" (John i. 10), "became flesh and dwelt among us" (John i. 14).

This comparison between the Greek and Hebrew beliefs about reality leads us to expect the difference which in fact we do find between the Classical and Biblical doctrines of man. In contrast with the Classical ideal of contemplative virtue, the supremacy of reason and the ultimate unworthiness of the body and manual activities, the Biblical ideal is of active righteousness; salvation is conceived of as involving the whole man, body and soul, and there is no discrimination against manual activity. The whole man is in need of salvation, because the whole world is in sin; but the whole man must enter into salvation.

The fact of chief importance to the theme of this chapter is that, broadly speaking, the educational thought of the modern world has been inspired by the Classical view of man as a rational animal, perfectible through the triumph of Reason, rather than by the Biblical doctrine of man as a fallen child of God, redeemable by Divine grace.

The Greek ideal of man as the perfect rational animal accounts for two apparently contradictory tendencies in Greek life and thought: on the one hand a keen appreciation of physical beauty and the cult of the body, and on the other hand the yearning of the spirit to free itself from the down-drag of the flesh. The latter tendency proceeds in fact from the perception, sometimes more and sometimes less conscious, which casts a shadow of ultimate pessimism over all the best of Greek thought, that the ideal of the perfect rational animal is an illusion and that there is a frustrating contradiction in man. "When does the soul attain to truth?" asks Socrates in the *Phaedo*. "It thinks best when . . . it takes leave of the body . . . and departs into the realm of the pure and the everlasting, the immortal and the changeless." The Greek tragedians, with deeper insight than the philosophers, knew that the naturalistic ideal is doomed to frustration; and it was in tragedy that the loftiest reach of the Greek spirit ended.

Disparagement of the body (which is closely associated with disparagement of manual labour) is essentially a pagan attitude. The Greeks, notwithstanding their interest in the body (and perhaps because of it), never achieved the Hebrew-Christian acceptance of the body as holy. Natural man, discovering in himself the tension between flesh and spirit—between man as animal and man as the image of the divine—can escape from the dilemma only by denying the flesh or denying the spirit—by asceticism or sensualism. Apart from redemption by divine grace, the noble man can escape from the dilemma only by condemning the flesh. Thus Plato and the best of the Greeks— and all noble pagans—see the body as ultimately unworthy.

The Hebrews on the other hand believed that the whole man was formed for God's service and could be redeemed as a whole.* If we turn to St. Paul, we find no prejudice against the body and manual labour. "Neither did we eat bread for nought at any

---

* The persistence in Christian theology of the doctrine of bodily resurrection is but a crude way of affirming this very important faith in the holiness of the whole man.

man's hand, but in labour and travail, working night and day, that we might not burden any of you" (2 Thess. iii. 8–10). And salvation was of the whole man including the body. "The whole creation groaneth . . . and we ourselves groan within ourselves waiting for the adoption, to wit the redemption of our bodies" (Rom. viii. 22–3). The Bible from beginning to end testifies to an *incarnate* notion of truth, in contrast with Plato's discarnate notion of truth. Truth to the Hebrew prophet is not something immutably beheld in the suspension of a sort of spiritual inter-stellar space, but is revealed through the process of history, wrung from the surge of life through intensity of experience. To the prophet the vision of God came in moments of social and political crisis; the incandescence of the eternal vision was produced by the friction of historical change. So Paul's famous and tremendous catalogue of personal sufferings and humiliations in 2 Corinthians xi. 23–30 rises to its great closing chord of "I must needs *glory*! . . . If so be that we suffer with Him, that we may be also glorified with Him."

Such a view of Truth and of salvation necessarily implies a general as well as a special doctrine of incarnation. The whole Biblical theme has its climax in the Person of Christ. But what is less often emphasized is that, had we only the Old Testament, we should still have a general philosophy of incarnation presented in a most varied literature extending over many centuries. And we should still see that philosophy of incarnation more and more clearly taking shape through prophetic interpretation of the actual process of history. It is a philosophy that takes history seriously as the material in terms of which the Eternal is revealed. God is made known in His works, and Truth is found in action. This belief in history as a medium of revelation and a mode of creation vibrates throughout the Bible, and is something to which the Greeks, notwithstanding they produced Herodotus and Thucydides, never attained. There is, in this view, none of the statuesque detachment of the Platonic Idea, but the warmth of God's activity in His world. It is a view that sets the concrete, the organic, the dynamic against the abstract, the analytical, the static. In this connection the theology of the Fourth Gospel is very important. The *Logos* (originally a Greek conception) was made flesh. This idea of the incarnation of the Logos was a boldly revolutionary step in thought, which could have occurred only in the context of Hebrew-Christian religious experience. The incarnational doctrine of the nature of Truth and of history also carries with it the sanctification of work. The belief that pure contemplation can lead to salvation is out of tune with the Biblical spirit. Truth is something to which one cannot *think* one's way but to which one has to *live* one's way. There is in fact a limitation about the purely speculative standpoint which precludes the attainment of truth.

To say that, however, does not dispose of the belief that thought is in some sense an end in itself. There is a nobility about pure thought which has to be acknowledged and needs explanation—a conviction that in the realm of pure thought man is most truly himself. The grounds of this conviction are perhaps to be found in the fact that man, who shares with the animals the power of mastering his environment by *manipulating* it, stands alone in his power to master his environment by *understanding* it. If deprived of all means of manipulation man can still rise above his situation intellectually and spiritually; he can be captain of his soul even if not master of his fate. In this sense there is, as Rousseau said, liberty in dungeons. That is what gives majesty to human thought, and is the ground of the belief in "liberal education" as something supra-practical. But there is a confusion of thought in this exaltation of thought above action. The uniquely human possibility of purely intellectual or spiritual mastery does not justify the voluntary rejection of the world of action and our responsibilities therein. That way lies the dualism of body and mind, with its implied condemnation of the body as evil and acceptance of the mind alone as good. The fact that man *can* operate in the field of pure thought does not constitute thought as an end in itself nor justify academic seclusion, philosophic abstraction, or even mystical ecstasy.* The true end of

---

* It will be remembered that St. Theresa of Avila, herself the subject of unsought mystical experiences, thus addressed a novice: "My daughter, we do not want ecstasies here; we want someone who can wash up."

thought is action. Truth, as was said, must be lived into, not only thought into. Intellectual activity is only justified, and ultimately profitable, in proportion as it interprets the world of experience and, passing beyond interpretation, flows back into action. "Withdrawal" is only valid when it is part of a whole rhythm of "withdrawal-and-return." No institution ought to be wholly withdrawn, and no individual ought to be withdrawn all the time.

This discussion of the Classical and Biblical views of Reality in relation to the world of forthcoming experience has educational implications which have been insufficiently appreciated. But, before going on to distinguish them, it is worth observing that the two traditions that have been contrasted have something very important in common.* They both affirm the existence of absolute values which are neither the projection of individual minds nor the product of the social process. None of the Greeks was able to reach a fully incarnational view of the relation between the Eternal and the world of experience, and therefore were unable to overcome the dualism of eternity and time, spirit and matter, soul and body, thought and action. But the Hellenic and Hebrew-Christian insights agree in acknowledging a Reality which is objective to the individual mind and transcends the historical process. Both insights therefore stand together against the modern relativism which disintegrates intellectual coherence and corrodes moral values.

Educational Implications

It only remains to make clear the relation between the discussion in this chapter and the argument in previous chapters about the reciprocal responsibility of school and community. If the function of culture is to interpret civilization, it can do so only when it is rooted in the life and work of the civilization which it is its business to interpret. Herein is the relation of thought to life, of the scholar to the general public, and educational

---

* The emphasis in this chapter has been on the contrast. No mention has been made, for example, of the medieval, Thomistic, synthesis of Aristotle and Christian theology.

institutions to the community at large. Broadly speaking the Classical tradition has tended to separate higher education from the daily life of the community, the scholar from the general public, while the Biblical tradition insists on the unity of thought and life, philosophy and work. The Biblical tradition, therefore, is implicit in all that was said earlier about the relation between school and community. That knowledge ought to be useful; that work in school ought as far as possible to be of direct value to the community; that the whole community ought to share in the work of education—such propositions as these clearly reflect the Biblical view of the relation of truth to life, thought to action. They implicitly deny the "ivory tower" conception of culture.

At the same time it would be misleading to suggest that the Classical tradition is repudiated. The proposition that the aim of society is the good life, and that education is the essential means of achieving the good life, would have had the full approval of Plato and Aristotle. The relation between the two traditions is far from being one of direct opposition; were that the case, Aquinas's synthesis would have been impossible. Rather, the Hebrew-Christian insight is deeper than the Hellenic and, through the idea of incarnation, resolves a dualism which always vitiated Greek thinking and which appears as a dichotomy of eternity and time, spirit and matter, thought and action, freeman and slave.

In terms of education, the incarnation of the Logos means a relationship between life and learning such that learning continually issues in action and people in their daily lives are continually aware of the principles which their actions seek to express. We have already seen something of what this implies for the school in its relations with the community in general. It is perhaps worth while to add something about the function of institutions for higher learning. The universities ought to be the intellectual power-stations of the community, and the work of the Arts faculties ought to have as vital a bearing on the life of the whole nation as the science faculties. Arts faculties are too often introverted and inclined to protect themselves with an insulating wrapping of arguments about "academic freedom," "pure scholarship," "learning for learning's sake," and so on; and the demand that academic studies should be planned with more regard for the actual concerns of the general public is rebuffed with references to "dilution" and "hauling down the flag." Yet the universities will not do their duty by the general public unless they pay serious attention to the forms of art and techniques of communication which interest and occupy the general public. Is it fanciful to imagine, for example, that the cinema and broadcasting might be as closely linked with research in the Arts faculties as research in the science faculties is linked with industrial manufacture?

On the other hand, it is no less important that the university should redeem every field of knowledge from a treatment that is merely technical. There is, fortunately, a good deal of opinion in this country for placing new technological departments within the universities rather than have them established directly under industrial and governmental control. The main reason for keeping technological development within the sphere of influence of the universities is in order that technologists may have the fullest opportunity of relating their specialized studies to a general philosophy of life.

Perhaps the most important obligation upon all university teachers at the present time is to make a serious effort, individually and in co-operation with one another, to discover and express the most coherent and effective philosophy of life of which they are capable. The most serious weakness of the universities at present is their depressing lack of belief and conviction about anything. There is a growing uneasiness among university teachers on account of the incoherence of the education offered to students. Committees confer on the problem of how a number of separate courses of instruction can somehow be made to grow into an education; and for the most part the discussion is content to explore the well-trodden avenues of syllabus-reform. The last place—because the most embarrassing—where university teachers will look for the source of the trouble is in themselves. To such an extent are we become victims of the modern relativism, in which there are no longer any universal and abiding values but everywhere a Heraclitean flux, that we no longer dare to acknowledge ends and values and ultimate judgments, but more and more busy ourselves with methodological problems. In this failure of morale we are apt to behave as if we were even more spiritually bankrupt than we are. If we would pull ourselves together we would still find in our tradition the elements of a faith worth living for. This is not the place to discuss the ultimate adequacy or inadequacy of the liberal humanism of our classical heritage. But this much at all events is clear: that the belief in Truth, Beauty, and Goodness as objective values, recognized but not constituted by the human mind, and in the sacredness of human personality and the essential freedoms that depend upon it, is a worthy faith as far as it goes and still has power to unite the great majority of people. If university teachers would recognize how much the world needs a common faith, and how much their teaching depends for its vitality upon a personal faith, they would find that the liberal humanist tradition is capable of positive and effective restatement.*

The higher learning fails in its social function equally if it does not issue in action and if it is not inspired by a coherent view of life. This relation of the higher learning to the life of society in general has its counterpart in the relation of an individual's academic studies to his function in the community. Education cannot take place *in vacuo*, and the term "well-educated" or "a good education" has meaning only in relation to some particular community and to some function in it. One can be a good plumber or a good doctor without being a good man; but it is impossible to be a good man without being a good plumber, doctor, engineer, shepherd, and so on. Herein is the true relation

* The teacher sometimes excuses himself from the responsibility for having a faith on the grounds that students ought not to be indoctrinated but ought rather to think out their own beliefs. Assuredly students ought not to be in-doctrinated—if indoctrinating means overriding the student's right and duty to do his own thinking. But the student's opportunity of forming positive and coherent beliefs depends to a great extent upon his encountering positive and coherent beliefs in his teachers and fellow-students. The student's choice of beliefs should be his own; but he is bound to choose from what comes within his experience. A prevailing atmosphere which is negative and sceptical is not only uninspiring in itself; it also provides a soil in which weeds flourish.

between the "liberal" and "vocational" principles. The liberal ideal is valuable in so far as it reminds us that men are more than their functions and that the function needs to be taken up into a philosophy and so redeemed from being merely toil or technique. No less necessary is it—as the vocational principle reminds us—that ideas, values, and personal qualities must become incarnate in activities which have their place in the life of the community. Incarnation and redemption are thus complementary aspects of the same thing.

Summary of Part I

This summary is intended as a convenient aid to the reader's memory and is therefore placed after the chapters to which it refers. It is not likely to be helpful to anyone who has not read the book.

Two formulæ are suggested at the outset (Chapter I) to describe the nature of education. Considered as the process by which the individual human being becomes the best that he is capable of becoming, education may be described as the nurture of personal growth. Considered as an instrument by which the community maintains itself, education may be described as the conservation, transmission, and renewal of culture.

An examination of the *personal* leads to the conclusion that the achievement of personal living (i.e. becoming a person in the full sense of the word) involves both freedom and community, and that the community of freedom is the association of persons in spontaneous fellowship (or love). Since the achievement of personal living in this sense is the highest purpose of life, it is the supreme aim of education. The process of self-fulfilment is seen to be frustrated if it is deliberately sought. It is rather a by-product of the life in which the self is lost in something more than self—persons grow by giving, not by getting—which is another way of saying what has been said about the relation between freedom, community, and love. This primary liberation from self (always in fact incomplete) depends on our being taken hold of, claimed or "redeemed," by something other than ourselves. Though the response must be our own, the otherness of that to which we respond is equally important.

An examination of the *historical* (Chapter III) throws fresh light on the nature of the personal and leads to the proposition that it is persons and not systems that are redeemed, i.e. while in the process of history some systems become impossible to maintain and are replaced by others (and there is a sense in which these changes are inevitable), it does not follow that a particular system holds the secret of human perfection, that mankind's problems can be solved by arriving at the right stage in historical development. What historical change certainly does is to alter the form in which man's essential problems present themselves; there is no evidence that it solves them. The quality of a society, and its approximation to perfection, depends ultimately on the personal qualities of its members—on the amount of spontaneous good will that exists to redeem the society. Theoretically *any* system could provide the context of the perfect community. In practice some systems are obviously more conducive under given conditions than others to the creation of perfect community. But there is no evidence to suggest that any system as such contains any guarantee of good or of evil.

Next (Chapter IV) comes an analysis of our contemporary world in order to arrive at the special aim of education for our time. This analysis leads to the conclusion that the gravest danger to our civilization is the undermining of personal values —the depersonalizing of human relations and the cheapening of the value set upon the individual human being. To some extent this is seen to be the result of industrialization and the growth of technology, creating a world that works better if most people are like machines. But the problem goes deeper than that and involves the dilemma in which modern man finds himself as a result of the assertion of the unfettered individual at the time of the Renaissance—the emancipation of modern man from the old authorities, intellectual and moral as well as political and economic. The tension between the individual and society has thus become very much more difficult to resolve in the modern world, since it can no longer be resolved at the semi-conscious level of custom. Modern man tends to seek escape from the dilemma either by denying responsibility (individualism) or by sacrificing liberty for the sake of security (collectivism). Either way, the true stature of personality is jeopardized, since persons can grow only when freedom and community are united. The special aim of education in our time is seen to be the general aim multiplied, as it were, by the peril in which personal values stand, and may be stated as the creation of freedom in the planned society. Since people are free in proportion as they do the right thing of their own accord, the redemption of the planned society must be essentially an educational achievement.

There follows a criticism of modern western education as reflecting the character of western culture in its preoccupation with techniques and the weakness of its grasp of ultimate meaning and purpose. In connection with the content of education, attention is drawn to the disintegration of thought and knowledge into separate, autonomous dominions, each a law unto itself with no overall view of life, comparable with the disintegration of the medieval *imperium* into a number of national sovereign states, and of the personal into groups of factors (e.g. the modern novel presents problems and functions rather than people). Further light is thus thrown on the nature of the personal; to become a person it is necessary to have a coherent view of life.

The next step is to apply these conclusions to the practical business of education. Three essential elements of modern education are distinguished—(i) A study of the world we live in; (ii) direct experience of community living; (iii) the "Vision of Greatness." Of these the first should illustrate the present danger to personal values, the second should give practical experience of personal values in action, and the third should supply the necessary inspiration.

A consideration of the relation between the school and the larger community (Chapter V) emphasizes the complementary needs (*a*) for the school to stretch out into the community and (*b*) for the community to enter into the business of education. The proposition that education ought to be the whole community in action is seen to have far-reaching implications, touching, e.g. the home, industry, public services. It is suggested that the most important function of the school in relation to society at large is to achieve such a measure of true fellowship as to present an object lesson in the meaning of community.

Finally (Chapter VI) there is an examination of the two main historical sources (the Hellenic or Classical and the Hebrew-Christian or Biblical) of our western culture and therefore of our educational tradition. Whereas these have in common the affirmation of absolute values, and are therefore both opposed to contemporary relativism, they are contrasted inasmuch as the Greek philosophers never overcame the dualism of spirit and flesh, thought and action, and believed contemplation to be the highest human activity and the body to be ultimately unworthy. Throughout the Bible, on the other hand, runs an incarnational view of Reality, in which Truth is revealed in and through the turmoil of history, thought must issue in action, and the body as well as the soul is holy and should be consecrated to the service of God. In terms of education the Biblical, or incarnational, view involves a relationship between life and learning such that learning continually issues in action and people in their daily lives are continually aware of the principles which their actions seek to express. This view is already implicit in what has been said of the relation of school and community—that knowledge ought to be useful, school work ought to be of value to the larger community, and the whole community ought to share in the work of education. The same doctrine is further illustrated from the field of higher education and there is some discussion of the function of the university, which needs at one and the same time to be more "functional" and also to have, among its teaching staff, a clearer and more coherent philosophy of life.

Part II

Christianity and Education

"For the Jews require a sign, and the Greeks seek after wisdom: but we preach Christ crucified, unto the Jews a stumblingblock, and unto the Greeks foolishness."

1 Cor., i. 22, 23.

" . . . and the world knew Him not."

John, i. 10.

VII

The Relevance of Christianity

THIS book is not, except by implication, an essay in Christian apologetics. The purpose of Part II is not to debate Christian doctrine, but to show that the Christian gospel and the Christian interpretation of history fulfil the obvious incompleteness of the analysis of man and his problems in Part I. Part I, while reaching some important conclusions about the nature of man and history, and the function of education, nevertheless leaves some large question-marks projecting, as it were, into space; there is no answer in Part I to the ultimate mystery and perpetual frustration of man. The object of the present chapter is to set the Christian answer against the human question. If, in the light of the Christian interpretation, the shadows of natural human anxiety and speculation are less impenetrable—if, on the Christian hypothesis, man and his world make sense where there was no sense before—that is at least presumptive evidence in favour of Christianity.

The Human Question

The analysis of man and his history, which occupied a good deal of Part I, presupposed nothing but normal human experience. Some words were used (such as "sin," "redemption," "incarnation") which belong to the vocabulary of Christian doctrine and are less commonly met with in secular discussion. But these words were used because they were believed to be the best words for their purpose, and not with the intention of imposing specifically theological interpretations at this stage. The following passage occurs in the preface to Sir Fred Clarke's *Freedom in the Educative Society*: "I trust readers will not be offended to find old-fashioned terms like conscience and discipline, duty and patriotism, sin and repentance deliberately employed. They are used because they are needed to indicate real forces that we can no longer shun or ignore. Any who may still object to the use of such terms as being 'reactionary' might ask themselves whether, in our eager progressiveness, we have not been throwing kernels into the dustbin and hoping to grow fat and lusty on the husks."* We have become strangely coy about such words as "sin" and "love." But the exclusion of these old words, and the substitution for them of paler, more scientific-sounding ones, impoverishes thought as well as expression. To take one example, the proposition that man needs redemption, which occurs early in Part I, is weakened by the use of some other word. "Redemption" ($\dot{a}\pi o\lambda\acute{v}\tau\rho\omega\sigma\iota s$), with its historical association of buying back a slave into freedom, means more than "liberation"; it implies liberation at some cost to the liberator, and thus conveniently relates liberation with love, which is the creator of freedom and suffers through the creation of freedom.

Man, it was argued, cannot make sense of himself simply as a superior animal. Inward conflict and contradiction are intrinsic, and there is no solution of man's problems at the level of the "natural." The inward contradiction, which appears in the tension between reason and instinct, appears also in the paradoxical experience that self-seeking defeats its own ends—that the conscious and deliberate pursuit of "happiness" or self-fulfilment, albeit at a high ethical level, is strangely self-frustrating —and that the first condition of the fulfilment of personal destiny is to be set free from self by being claimed and taken possession of by something more than self, in which the self is lost but which gives back the self enriched. The term "sense of sin" was used to denote the realistic recognition of the contradiction within man, from which he needs to be "redeemed." And attention was drawn to the important distinction between, on the one hand, the healthy acknowledgment of the fact of "sin" and the need for redemption, and, on the other hand, the morbid inhibition (which the psychologists call "guilt") resulting from a disinclination to face facts. A proper sense of sin never inhibited anybody; it is in fact the first step to any resolution of the

* P. 10. Most of Part I had been written before I read this book of Sir Fred Clarke's.

tensions which, if allowed to pile up internally, give rise to "guilt."* There are three alternative courses open to anyone who is oppressed by the sense of contradiction and frustration. He can face facts by acknowledging his inadequacy and need of help in resolving the tension ("repentance"). Redemption consists in the release from preoccupation with self and reorganization of life about a new centre which is not self. Secondly, he can refuse, through fear and pride, to face facts, and his life becomes a deceit, haunted by feelings of guilt. Thirdly, he may escape from the tension, not through its resolution but through its repression. In this way an apparent serenity, or complacency, is reached, but there will be the familiar symptoms of compensation—a camouflage of scrupulousness about less important things. Writing of the inevitability of moral tension in the growth of personality, Sir Fred Clarke has this to say about the first and third of the alternatives just distinguished: "Central to the whole structure is the *moral* tension which characterizes the free man of goodwill. They are probably right who find in a weakening of the sense of this tension, and of its central importance, a source of much of the confusion and positive evil of our own times. There is no more vivid illumination of the crucial significance of it than that which is provided by the contrast between the Pharisee and the publican in the parable. In the one all tension has gone, unable to hold out against his inordinate self-approval, and he is left unconscious of his own utter flabbiness, however proudly he may stand. In the other, tension is at maximum stretch. Aware at last of the magnitude of the gulf between the majesty of his human calling and the ignominy of his achievement, he can only repeat 'God be merciful to me, a sinner!' Yet it was he who was 'justified,' we might say, who attained to full sanity. For the measure of moral tension in this sense is the measure of the true self-awareness and so of sanity."†

* Common experience confirms this distinction. A "guilty" manner denotes anxiety lest one should be found out and a desire not to be found out—i.e. a desire to hide one's offence. If one makes a clean breast of it, one is no less a sinner, but one is no longer in retreat from oneself. If confession is met with forgiveness and renewed trust (i.e. love), the sinner is, in a measure at least, "redeemed."

† *Freedom in the Educative Society*, pp. 62–63.

The contradiction in human life was seen again in the difficulty of reconciling in practice the claims of individuality and the claims of community. Ideally this tension is resolved in a social relationship in which the individual, giving himself without reserve to the community, receives himself again fulfilled. Such a service is freedom. But service is freedom only within a relationship of fellowship or love; and natural man seems incapable of creating such fellowship. If, on the one hand, actual individuals are incapable of giving themselves without reserve, so, on the other hand, no actual community is a fit object of unqualified devotion. Thus, for example, the individual must always in some sense protect himself against the state, and the state can never have an absolute claim on the individual. And so again there appears the need for redemption—of communities as well as of individuals.

The ideal fellowship in which service is freedom may be described as a community whose purpose is the personal fulfilment of all its members. But when individuals serve a community whose purpose is something else—such as the self-interest of a powerful group—the result of loyalty and devotion will not be the fulfilment but the exploitation and ultimate destruction of the deluded victims. That is obvious. But the converse of this situation is worth considering—that is to say, the redeeming power of love, whether it be of parents, friends, or a community, and whether sought or unsought. It is a commonplace that children need love in order to grow as persons, and that lack of love is a fatal spiritual starvation, though children so starved may not know what it is that they lack. What is true of children is true of people of all ages. To discover that one is valued for one's own sake by someone who at the same time is under no illusions about one is more likely than any other experience to bring out the best in one. If we are taken into fellowship (i.e. loved) we are not only comforted; we are challenged. If we respond to the challenge by loving as we are loved, we are in that measure liberated and fulfilled. If we refuse to respond (and it is of the nature of love to leave us free to refuse) our own hearts will condemn us and we shall know no peace.

Common experience can furnish plenty of illustrations of the redemptive power of the love of individuals, and in human affairs the love of a mother must stand as the type of such redeeming love. We can also find some evidence of the redeeming power of a community. But this naturally tends to be greatest in small communities which are held together by personal affection (e.g. families) and least in large, impersonal communities (e.g. nations), in which the bond of union can only in a figurative sense be described as love.

All these reflections point to man's need for redemption by love, and the question left on our hands is whether man is capable of supplying, from his individual and social resources, the redemptive power necessary for the solution of the great human problems of domestic, industrial, and international relations.

There are two reasons why we must be at least very doubtful whether a purely this-worldly view of life, in terms of human resources, can supply the answer to man's problems—why, that is to say, we must be very sceptical of the contemporary dogma of human self-sufficiency.

Empirically, the evidence of history does not encourage a belief in human perfectibility within the frame of history. If we can infer any general law of development, it is one of increasing potentiality for both good and evil, and of increasing tension between them. It is true, if the analysis in Part I is accepted, that man in an important sense transcends the time-process and that, the more truly personal the level on which life is lived, individually and collectively, the more man can act upon history instead of being acted upon by history—the more man can live at the level of decision rather than of mere causation. But the development of civilization does not in fact suggest the attainment of man's mastery of his fate. Rather, we behold the undermining of personal values, the spectacle of modern man gaining the whole world and losing his own soul. We see that modern man has, by raising the essential problem of social relations to a higher level, made it vastly more difficult to solve; and we see him trying to escape from the dilemma into more than one kind of frustration. Meanwhile he clings in desperation to the dogma of human self-sufficiency and thus paradoxically combines increasing uneasiness about the state of civilization with obstinate complacency about man. This refusal to seek the cause of failure in man himself is the essence of "sin."

It might be argued that inferences about the fate of man in history ought not to be drawn from a single civilization which has so obviously gone wrong. But, if our own civilization has gone wrong, history cannot show any civilization that has gone right; and there is certainly a good deal of evidence to suggest that decline is as intrinsic to the pattern of civilization as growth. It is worth reminding ourselves, moreover, that recent exploration into the nature of man and of history has done a good deal to upset the Renaissance faith in man and the nineteenth-century belief in progress; and that this exploration has been the work of non-Christians and anti-Christians. In a recent broadcast debate,* Professor H. A. Hodges pointed out that it was Karl Marx who said that institutions and systems contain within themselves the seeds of their own destruction, and that Sartre and the existentialists are breaking the Renaissance idol by their insistence that man must ruthlessly plumb his own depths and see himself stripped of all his illusions. If civilization is a mess and man cuts a sorry figure, the Christians are by no means alone in saying so. And modern man, in clinging to the dogma of human self-sufficiency, is "whistling to keep up his spirits."

If human history gives us little ground for expecting the achievement of the perfect society,† a consideration of man's deepest problems does not lead us to think that they can be solved in terms of this world. If we accept a view of life in which human personality is the supremely valuable thing, and the purpose of life is the embodiment and expression, by persons, of all that is true and beautiful and good, then we must

---

* The third of a series of debates between Professor H. A. Hodges and Vernon Mallinson on "Clearing the Ground: Can Christianity satisfy the need of modern man for a faith to live by?"

† It is significant that Marxism has to resort to apocalyptic for the final scene of the drama. The social revolution, with all the apparatus of dictatorship which many communists deplore, results fairly and squarely from historical causes. But the eventual emergence of the classless society and the withering away of the state scarcely belong to the same realm of reality.

ask the question which Socrates asked: whether the world in which these values have their being is this transitory world of space and time alone; and, if so, whether man can face his destiny with any feeling nobler or more hopeful than resignation. In other words, we have got to reckon with the fact of death— the death of men and women, the death of fellowship and love, the disintegration of all constructions of hand and brain, and the decay of all earthly things. If Death is the conqueror, and all man's hopes and fears, achievements and failures, sublimities and ignominies, all end in the same cosmic dust, then human existence is a joke in very poor taste—or would be if we could imagine a cosmic Joker—and the only possible philosophies for man would be stoicism or hedonism.

Man's deepest questions remain unanswered unless there is some reality for him which goes beyond death, which the forces of this world are powerless to destroy, and which gives more than ironical meaning to the yearnings of the spirit. The soul of man must face defeat and annihilation—that is ultimate meaninglessness—unless there is something from which "neither death nor life, nor angels nor principalities nor powers, nor things present nor things to come, neither the height above nor the depth beneath, nor anything else in creation"* can separate him, and in the security of which he need not fear what man can do to him.† Nothing in this world, no devotion to a person or a cause, can have that transcendent and indestructible quality.

The Christian Answer

The doctrine of the Fall is not a Hebrew-Christian invention. That man is a creature at odds with himself and is his own worst enemy, and that the best human systems contain the germs of their own corruption—this is universal human experience. The difference between Christians and non-Christians is this: whereas non-Christians find the self-contradictory nature of man mystifying and embarrassing, Christians take firm hold of it and make it explain everything else. In the Christian interpretation this central fact about man does not baffle but illuminates.

* Romans, viii. 38, 39.   † Psalms, lvi. 4, cxviii. 6.

The view of man as a superior kind of animal leaves out everything about man that really interests him—everything that exalts him to the heights and casts him into the depths. Christianity recognizes that the most important thing about man is that he is made in God's image—that he is a creator* in his own right. In other words, man has freedom, and his freedom is the source of the best and the worst in him and of the conflict between them. Although a creator, man is also creature, and his true nature is to create within the conditions of his creatureliness. If he denies and rebels against his creatureliness he violates the laws of his being and defeats himself. But, since his freedom is real and not only a semblance, he does rebel against his creatureliness and tries to make himself free *from* God instead of free *for* God. The conflict in man is the revolt of the divine in man against the laws of his being, and this Promethean revolt is the essence of "sin." Sin is thus not merely the display of an inferior side of man's nature; it is the corruption of the best in man. It is for this reason that man cannot rescue himself from sin but needs redemption. Without redemption by the grace of God, man's noblest spiritual attainment is tragedy. The essence of tragedy is that in the height of his aspiration man falls to the depths, and yet when fallen he can tower in spirit over his ruin.†

It is the love of God that can rescue man from that ultimate tragedy which, however noble, is none the less ruin. As it is love that creates freedom, so it is love alone that can redeem the misuse of freedom. Seen in this light, sin is the rejection of love, the denial of our need of it. There is nothing mysterious about this sequence in which love creates freedom, freedom is abused, and love is again needed to redeem the misuse of freedom. If it is the theme of the universe, it is also the theme of the family, and every mother knows that it is true. Where there is no love, no freedom is given, because it is always less trouble not to give freedom. Only love undertakes the anxiety and responsibility of giving freedom. Freedom is inevitably abused, because we have

* As artist, philosopher, statesman, inventor, and so on.
† See my *Education—Christian or Pagan*, p. 78. The whole of Chapter V of that book may be found useful as a fuller discussion of the Christian doctrine of man.

to learn how to use it, and until we have learnt we are irresponsible, inconsiderate, destructive, selfish. The abuse of freedom brings grief to the giver. And in the long run only more love can win back the heart (not only the outward behaviour) of the selfish and destructive to considerate responsibility. This is both homely experience and sound Christian doctrine. Neither creation nor freedom can be without suffering. God could have saved Himself and us a great deal of trouble by making a world of insects.

Because man is free, there can be nothing coercive about God's redemption. Conviction of sin and repentance—the act by which man lays himself open to God's grace—must be man's own free and responsible act. Once he has made it and yielded his self-will to God's will, God can take him and remake him, bringing him into the new life which has God and not self for its centre.

In order to save, God enters the world—enters history. Attention has already been drawn to the fact that, throughout the Bible, God is an active God, working in history, and that the revelation of Himself in Christ, though a unique event, is not an isolated event, but is of a piece with the whole process of revelation of which it is the climax. We also saw that a general doctrine of incarnation (i.e. the belief that Reality is both transcendent and immanent, and truth is to be found in history and experience, not in abstraction from the world) has a good deal to commend it in that, at the price of paradox, it avoids absolutism (in which this world is unreal and illusory) and relativism (in which there is no reality more permanent than this transitory scene). We observed that the Greeks never achieved a fully "incarnational" view of reality, though they approached it; and, because they did not attain it, they never overcame the dualism of thought and action, spirit and matter, eternity and time. We recognized, moreover, that the incarnational view of reality has certain educational implications which commend themselves, including the essential unity of thought and action, and the principle that all knowledge ought to be useful and issue in action.

The special doctrine of Incarnation, which is the heart of the Christian gospel, presupposes the general doctrine of incarnation. It is possible to take an incarnational view of the nature of reality and not to be a Christian. But it is impossible to be a Christian without taking an incarnational view of reality. The revelation of God in Christ cannot mean anything unless it is a special instance—the supreme instance—of something that is going on all the time: unless, that is to say, it explains the true nature of all reality and all experience. If a religion claims to be true it must make sense of the whole of life, and life must make more sense in the light of it than without. It is of the greatest importance to understand that religious truth is not a special kind of truth, nor religious experience a queer, unnatural kind of experience belonging to some strange and other world. Religious experience is normal experience, and we have religious experience every day, whether or not we recognize it as such. Religious truth is normal experience understood at full depth; what makes truth religious is not that it relates to some abnormal field of thought and feeling but that it goes to the roots of the experience which it interprets.

The Christian teaching about Christ must be seen, therefore, in its relation to all man's problems and perplexities, hopes and fears, and needs. Too often the secular historian's attitude to the life of Jesus suggests that he has here encountered something embarrassingly out of shape with the rest of history, something that has to be either tactfully ignored or industriously explained away. In one sense, of course, Christ *is* outside history—inasmuch as He measures history and is not measured by it. But it is equally true and important that He reveals the inward meaning of history, and measures history by so doing. The Incarnation is the supreme revelation of the nature of God in so far as God can be revealed in terms of human life, and is also a unique revelation of the possibilities of man when wholly at one with God as Father. "He came into the world—the world that was made through Him—yet the world knew Him not. He came to His own home; yet His own folk received Him not." The Cross is thus at one and the same time the supreme meaning of history and the supreme judgment of history; it cannot be the one without the other.

This very slight indication of the Christian teaching about man and the redeeming power of God in Christ is far from being an adequate statement of the subject for readers who want an introduction to the essentials of the Christian faith. There are a good many books which such readers would find helpful.* The purpose of the foregoing sketch, together with the preceding summary of the relevant arguments of Part I, is only to afford grounds for the conclusion that Christian doctrine *completes* rather than *displaces* the natural interpretation of experience. The contradictory nature of man and his inability to fulfil his destiny by his own natural resources, his need of redemption, the power of love to redeem, and the relation between creation, freedom, suffering, and love—we do not need to go to the theologian to learn of these things, for universal human experience tells us continually, though imperfectly, of them. The interpretation of life that the Bible and Christian doctrine give us is not *different* from the natural meaning of life but is complete where the other is incomplete. Without the Christian Gospel, man is left with the unsolved riddle of his destiny. "The good that I would, I do not; and the evil that I would not, that I do." Man knows that he needs redemption and that he cannot redeem himself. He does not know whether there is any power beyond him to save him—whether beneath him is the abyss or the everlasting arms. The Christian Gospel shows him that the theme of creation—freedom—sin—redeeming love, to which the world of nature and human experience gives obscure expression, is indeed the grand theme of the universe, that God is creative and redemptive Love and is, in Christ, reconciling the world to Himself; and that human life and human history can be fully

---

* The following are recommended for introductory reading: N. Micklem; *The Creed of a Christian* (S.C.M.); J. S. Whale: *This Christian Faith* (S.C.M.); A. Vidler: *A Plain Man's Guide to Christianity* (Heinemann); F. R. Barry: *What has Christianity to say?* (S.C.M.); W. Temple: *The Christian Faith and Life* (S.C.M.); W. Temple: *Christ's Revelation of God* (S.C.M.). Rather more advanced are Alan Richardson's *Christian Apologetics* (S.C.M.), and the late Canon Quick's admirable book *The Doctrines of the Creed* (Nisbet). Edwyn Bevan's *Christianity* (H.U.L.) is a very good survey of the history of Christianity.

9—(E.447) 24 pp.

understood only when brought to the feet of Christ and seen in the light of His countenance.

By virtue of thus completing or fulfilling the intimations of natural experience, the Christian Gospel makes much more sense of life. It gives meaning to much that is otherwise obscure and perplexing, and, as was suggested earlier, it boldly takes hold of the most frustrating of life's mysteries and makes them explain everything else. The self-contradictoriness of man becomes the key to God's plan for human freedom. Sin, as the consequence of freedom, has its full positive significance in the scheme of things and does not need to be explained away. Love appears in its full meaning as the greatest power in the universe—power to create, to suffer, and to redeem. Creative suffering is the warfare of love against its rejection, and this theme is apparent in history as well as in personal life. More will be said in a later chapter about the Cross as the meaning of history and the judgment of history. Whether in personal life or in the history of civilization, the Christian interpretation reckons fully with the failure of man and has no need to disguise or explain away that failure. And yet Christianity, alone of those philosophies which face the facts, is ultimately optimistic. It was the cheerfulness of the early Christians which, very understandably, most infuriated their persecutors. In the last resort the Christian who is possessed by Christ possesses in himself something which no power on earth, death not excepted, can destroy. This does not mean that the Christian is indifferent to the affairs of this world. There is nothing like Hindu or Buddhist world-renunciation about the Christian life. The body is the vehicle of the spirit, and the world is the workshop in which God's work has to be done. And not the least important part of God's work is feeding the hungry and clothing the naked. But the world is not our home, and the Christian can cheerfully count the world well lost for Christ. If this essentially Christian position (that the world matters supremely and yet matters not at all) seems too baffling a paradox, it is perhaps helpful to desist from the vain attempt to convey in words what is much more clearly revealed in the lives of persons. Persons in their living often explain what words obscure. A study of St. Paul's life and letters will teach us more about Christian discipleship than any amount of academic exposition, and we can re-inforce the lesson by studying the lives of the great disciples of other ages and of our own time.*

Christianity not only does not deny natural truth but transforms it by turning the tragedy of man into the triumph of God. It must be recognized, however, that Christian truth, illuminating as it is of all the dark places, is the truth of paradox. Christianity is paradoxical in that, while affirming man's need of salvation, it yet requires man's active seeking as a condition of grace; and paradoxical in that, while it takes this world seriously as the proper field of spiritual activity and growth, and history as the true revelation of reality, it nevertheless contemplates the fulfilment of man's destiny only beyond history, in the dimension of eternity (meaning "timeless" rather than "at the end of time"). And above all is the central paradox of the Cross, in which the powers of this world are finally defeated in the moment of their apparent victory. "We preach Christ Crucified, unto the Jews a stumbling block and unto the Greeks foolishness; but unto them that are called . . . Christ the power of God and the wisdom of God. Because the foolishness of God is wiser than men; and the weakness of God is stronger than men."†

But here again we must observe that Christianity does not import into the world of familiar experience a new and strange kind of truth, but rather fulfils the incompleteness of natural experience. The discrepancy between man's vision and his powers of performance is part of his nature and destiny; and so is the law that he must lose his life to find it. If life itself is paradoxical it is unreasonable to expect that the true interpretation of life will explain the paradox away. There are such interpretations for those who like them. Hindu mysticism, for example, by denying reality to the world of space and time, presents a

* George Seaver's *Albert Schweitzer—the Man and his Mind* (A. & C. Black) is a most interesting account of one of the great dedicated lives of our generation.

† 1 Cor. i. 23–25. Cf. 2 Cor. xii. 9: "My strength is made perfect in weakness." It is worth remembering the difficulty that Jesus had in convincing His intimate followers that He was not the kind of Messiah that contemporaries expected—i.e. He would not be a political success.

philosophy which is much more logically coherent than Christianity. The trouble is that, in relieving us from the burden of paradox, it relieves us of everything else as well, except the cold comfort of absorption into the Infinite, which is a polite name for extinction. Christianity does not explain life by eliminating those elements which most need explanation. On the contrary, Christianity accepts the paradox of experience together with its fullest implications, and uses it to show us that we have been mystifying ourselves by asking the wrong question. Christianity explains life, not by answering our questions in our way, but by making us change our own standpoint towards the experience which we are trying to interpret.

An analogy may help to make clear what is meant. The question often asked about telepathy: "How can an idea pass out of one mind into another?" assumes that minds are separate receptacles. If we assume that there is a common mental content below the level of consciousness, comparable with the subterranean intercommunication of volcanic peaks, the fact of telepathy is no longer perplexing, and the right question to ask is: "Why is telepathy not going on all the time?" Similarly, our question: "Why does man contradict and frustrate himself?" assumes that the true nature of man is self-perfectible. Only on this assumption is human experience perplexing, just as the bending of light is perplexing only when we assume that it always travels in straight lines. If, instead, we make the self-contradictoriness of man our basic assumption, and accept the implications of man's inability to perfect himself and his need of redemption, the whole situation is, as it were, turned inside out and the impenetrable cloud becomes the source of light. The original problem becomes the solution of the problem.

What the new perspective does is not to eliminate paradox but to show us that, once we reach a certain depth of insight, there can be no acceptable presentation of truth which does not involve paradox. For example, it is in the nature of love that ever closer union results in the strengthening, not the dissolution, of personal identity. But we do not deepen our understanding of life by rejecting that truth because, viewed as an academic proposition, it is self-contradictory. Rather, we deepen our understanding by accepting it as fully as possible with our whole being, at all levels of experience, so that it becomes a lamp to light our path. And in that light we can see that the uniqueness of Christianity among religions consists in the fact that the relationship between God and man is preserved from start to finish as a relationship of persons, and the transcendence of God and the freedom of man are thus held together in the central fact of the Incarnation.

Additional Note
Art and Personality in Relation to Christ

It was pointed out in an earlier chapter that a person is "free" in proportion as he is able to act at the level of responsible decision instead of being acted upon at the level of cause-and-effect. There is also, in this kind of behaviour, an identification of the self with the action, so that the person enters fully into what he does, takes full responsibility for it, and authenticates it as his own.

It was also observed that this quality of behaviour is distinctive of the activity of the artist. The artist puts the whole of himself into his work, and identifies himself with it as a unique, personal creation. Art is the affirmation of the self acting freely. This may only be true, however, of the artist's behaviour *as artist*. It is as artist that he attains the fully personal plane. As a human being in other situations of life he may be as imperfectly developed as his neighbours. But, if a man were to attain the fully personal level in everything that he did, his whole life would have the quality that we recognize in a work of art—the identity of the man with his work (in this case his life-work), the perfect wholeness of the personality, free and responsible in his command of self and situation.

If this analysis is true, is it not of some help to us in seeking to understand the perfection of the personality of Jesus and the "authority" with which He taught, and the difference of stature between Him and other men?

In the person of Jesus we can also find a supreme illustration of another property of personality which was observed in a previous chapter—namely the power of personal life to reveal truth by embodying it, and thus presenting, as it were, an argument above argument, silencing the disputation that obscures truth.

The identification of Jesus with His Father is the sustained theme of Chapters XIV–XVII of St. John's Gospel, and is there shown to be the condition of Jesus' power to reveal God to man. "I am in the Father, and the Father in me." "He that hath seen me hath seen the Father." "I am the way, the truth, and the life."

VIII
Christianity and History

CHRISTIANS would claim that Christianity alone makes history intelligible, that no other interpretation can hold Christ in the context of history and do justice both to history as the cradle and Cross of Christ, and to Christ as the meaning and measure of history.

The Nature of Historical Interpretation

Before discussing a particular interpretation of history, it would be wise to consider the nature of historical interpretation in general. History is susceptible to many different interpretations; and, although some of these are more adequate than others, it is clearly impossible to demand the universal acceptance of one philosophy of history as being the only one that is true, and the rejection of all others as being altogether erroneous. We must acknowledge, not only that different interpretations each contain at least some truth, but also that history is in a sense a mirror in which we see our own faces reflected, so that our judgment is always at the same time history's judgment of us, just as we cannot judge a painting or a piece of music without submitting ourselves to judgment by implication.* We must therefore ask the question: In what sense is an interpretation of history "true"; and how can we judge of its truth? Since history is essentially concrete and unique, it is obvious that an interpretation cannot be subjected to the kind of proof that is appropriate in the case of experimental science or a proposition of Euclid. Proofs in experimental science are possible only in so far as events are *not* unique; there could be no law of the expansion of gases unless gases could be relied upon to behave always in the same way under the same

* Bishop Creighton in a letter of 1st September, 1871, records this story told of Northcote. A critic superciliously remarked of a painting by Reynolds: "I don't see much in it." Northcote retorted: "Sir, if there wasn't more in it than you can see, there would be very little indeed."

conditions. But history does not repeat itself. And, although historical situations may be sufficiently comparable to justify inferences of the kind that make up Machiavelli's political sagacity, the essence of the historical is its once-for-all character; the same path is never trodden twice, the process is irreversible, and events cannot be reproduced at will under laboratory conditions. Similarly, we cannot expect, in historical interpretation, the kind of logical demonstration that is used in Euclid. Euclid deals with pure abstractions and can therefore proceed by formal reasoning upon certain agreed assumptions; the conclusions are untrue of any actual situation because there are no true points, straight lines, or triangles in real life. In real life every triangle is different from every other triangle, as is every historical event, and nothing can be postulated about all of them except that they are all triangles and all different.

It is clear that an altogether different approach is needed in judging the "truth" of an interpretation of history. It is, in fact, a different kind of truth that we are judging—a kind of truth much more akin to artistic truth than to scientific or logical truth. We should estimate the adequacy of a philosophy of history more as we would estimate the quality of a work of art. That is to say, we should esteem that interpretation to be most "true" which is most revealing, most charged with meaning. This kind of judgment is admittedly very personal, and depends a good deal on the eye of the beholder. It need not, however, be purely and uncritically intuitive. There are rational principles from which guidance can be had. Most important, perhaps, is what may be called the principle of comprehensiveness. The interpretation that accounts for more data is better than one that accounts for less. And the interpretation that does justice to an awkward piece of data is better than one that merely explains it away. For example, suppose that, of two interpretations A and B, B accounts for certain data. If A accounts for the same data, and for some other data ignored by B, and also accounts for interpretation B within the whole picture, then A is more adequate than B. For example, it might be claimed for Christianity that it accounts for the data which Marxism accounts for and for a good deal which Marxism fails to account for, including Marxism itself;* and that it does justice to Marxism (by disclosing its truth as well as its error), whereas Marxism fails to take the measure of Christianity and explains it only by explaining it away.

The Christian Interpretation of History

History is not merely a *process* like the evolution of a zoological species; it is a *drama* of personal forces, and can be fully understood only as drama. If that is so, our first concern must be to identify the main plot. "The most obvious meaning of history," writes Dr. Niebuhr, "is that every nation, culture and civilization brings destruction upon itself by exceeding the bounds of creatureliness which God has set upon all human enterprises."† If the Christian interpretation of history were bounded by the historical scene, there would be nothing more to be said. History would be the tragedy of man. But, because the Christian interpretation of history goes beyond history—and moreover affirms that history will never make sense unless seen from a standpoint beyond history—history is also the victory of God. In other words, a view of history that goes beyond history has this advantage over all interpretations that are enclosed by history, that it can *make sense of the failure of history* instead of seeing it as unintelligible frustration.‡ We have already considered the "incarnational" view of history in its general form. We now have to see what it becomes in its specifically Christian form, focused and fulfilled in Christ.

The heart of the drama is revealed in the Cross. The theme

* It has often been pointed out that Marxism ought to apply its own principle of interpretation to itself so as to give us a Marxist analysis of Marxism. A good deal more of Marxism would survive a Christian analysis than would survive a Marxist analysis.

† *The Nature and Destiny of Man*, Vol. I, p. 150.

‡ Those who believe that man can perfect human society within history have all the evidence against them, and are driven into the contradiction of making assumptions about human reason and natural virtue which render the failure of history still more difficult to account for. The classic instance of this fallacy is in Rousseau. Man is naturally good, and the conglomeration of iniquity known as civilization is the fault of history. Therefore let us do away with history and go back to nature. But who made history? If man is naturally good, how did he become so bad?

of history is man's misuse of the freedom created by God's love. History is the tragedy of freely given Love.* The Cross is what human freedom has done with God's love. And the drama ends, or seems to end, with the powers of this world in possession.

But there is more even than this in the claim that Christ Crucified is the key to the meaning of history. The Cross is not the end. The continual warfare of Love against its rejection does not end in the darkness of Golgotha. The ultimate victory of Love is beyond history, but the assurance of that victory is in history. Whether or not we choose to take the Gospel stories of the Resurrection literally, there is no escape from the fact that something tremendous happened to the little band of men, who, after their ignominious flight to the north, came back a few weeks later, and made the astonishing assertion, within a few hundred yards of the place of burial, that their Master was alive. The power of the Resurrection was released into history, and the Christian Church was born. By accepting utter defeat as the world reckons defeat, Christ lifts the whole situation out of the mundane stream of events into another spiritual clime, from which there is a secondary impact upon history far more potent than any worldly forces. The Kingdom that is not of this world has done more to change the world than any of the powers of this world.† "God hath chosen the weak things of the world to confound the things that are mighty."‡

If the theme of history is the creation of human freedom, the abuse of that freedom in man's illusion of self-sufficiency and self-perfectibility, and the assurance within history of the possibility of redemption, how is that theme worked out? It is worked out on many different scales—in the life of an individual, in a

* Berdyaev: "To understand the interior relationship between God and man as a drama of freely given love is to lay bare the sources of history." *The Meaning of History*, p. 53. "The freedom of evil . . . forms the real foundation of history." *Ibid.*, p. 77.

† It is interesting and valuable to read what A. J. Toynbee has to say on this theme in his *A Study of History*. In developing his thesis that the "gentle" reaction is in the long run more powerful in history than the "violent" reaction, he speaks of "a Kingdom of God which is not in time at all but is in a different spiritual dimension, and which, just by virtue of this difference of dimension, is able to penetrate our mundane life and transfigure it." *Abridged Edition*, p. 438.

‡ 1 Cor. i. 27.

family, in the transformation of economic and political systems, and in the rise and fall of civilizations. Always there are the seeds of corruption in the best of human enterprises, and always in failure and disaster there is the promise of eternal possibility. History contains many dramas, all variations on the theme. But the whole of history is also a single drama on the same theme. And if we look at history as a whole, the plainest fact about it is that the Cross divides history so that the modern world stands apart from the world before Christ. The coming of Christ changed the world in ways that cannot be ignored even by those who want to minimize His historical importance. The world could never be the same again, because in Christ there was not only a revelation of God but also a revelation of man— a revelation of man which rendered explicit certain things that had been only implicit in the ancient world. It is the making explicit of these things that gives the modern world its character of turbulence, swift movement, increasing tensions, and gathering sense of impending catastrophe.

The modern world originates with Christianity, and its keynote is the affirmation of the divinity of man. That is the source from which our unique civilization has sprung—a civilization which is distinguished from all others by two things: the ethical value set upon human personality as such* and the application of the human intellect to the systematic mastery of nature. And it is important to realize that the ethical valuation of the individual and the spirit of experimental science† both have their pre-Christian roots in the Hebrew culture.

* The idea that there are rights and obligations attaching to human beings as such, irrespective of status, never clearly emerged in the classical world. To Greeks and Romans there were rights pertaining to a freeman and rights pertaining to a slave. The conception of Rights of Man could not have arisen except in a Christian context. This is true notwithstanding the fact that the rights of man have sometimes been championed by people who acknowledged no debt to Christianity.

† Arnold Nash, in *The University and the Modern World*, has pointed out that the Hebrew temper is more conducive than the Greek to the development of experimental science. The Hebrews believed in the goodness of Creation whereas the Greek philosophers despised the temporal world. The Hebrews believed in doing rather than in merely knowing, and their notion of history was dynamic (i.e. change was expected and was felt to be significant). Greek science was intellectualistic, and the prejudice against manual labour inhibited experimental work.

The development of science and its application to industry and life in general are not in themselves evils. On the contrary, all knowledge is good provided that it is used to the glory of God. During the Middle Ages the Christian Church tried to contain the leaping enterprise of the human spirit within the bonds of piety, but did so by restricting the legitimate activity of the human spirit. The inevitable explosion occurred, and the Renaissance asserted the creative freedom of man made in the divine image and forgot that man is also a fallen creature. The result was the release into the modern world of the whole terrific force of human enterprise unsanctified in its presumptuous self-sufficiency. The hold of religion on men's minds weakened; man's material achievement gathered momentum while the creeping doubt about man himself eats into his confidence. Having lost faith in the power of the human spirit to transform situations from within, man desperately grasps at the hope of transforming man from the outside by the manipulation of circumstances and systems. He has gained the whole world and lost his own soul.

Christ came when the world was ready for the Christian revelation. Greek philosophy had asked all the essential questions about man in his relation to the universe and to his fellows, and Greek culture had demonstrated the possibilities and limitations of the human mind. Eastern mysticism had experimented with salvation through the denial and renunciation of the material world. Roman imperial government had provided western civilization with a system of law and the foundation of a world state. Meanwhile the Hebrew prophets had revealed the meaning of history as a drama of divine activity. The deepest Hebrew insight had reached the vision of the transformation of history by spiritual power from within rather than by political force from without, but this conception of the suffering Messiah (and of the corresponding Messianic function of Israel in history) had not overcome the incorrigibly political idea of their destiny which prevailed among the Jews, notwithstanding the repeated disasters that overtook their nationalistic ambitions. By the end of the pre-Christian era the Mediterranean world was in a state of *malaise* through a failure of the sources of spiritual energy. Greece was no longer creative. Rome had never created anything spiritual, and in Judea no prophet had spoken for two hundred years. Either Mediterranean civilization must collapse or some quite fresh spiritual power must enter into it. Yet all the means for the creation of a renewed civilization were present in the heritage of the Mediterranean world.

Into that situation came with explosive force the Christian revelation about man—that man is of infinite value in the universe and that the human spirit can turn the world upside down. The ancient world had been a world which man accepted rather than hoped to remake, and fate prevailed over the human will. That the Christian revelation about man was indissolubly bound up with the Christian revelation about God, and that man cannot remake the world unless God remakes man, was not only the most important part of the Christian Gospel but also the part most easily forgotten by modern man. The medieval attempt to hold all human activity within a religious synthesis was at its best a precarious equilibrium, and succeeded as much by cramping human invention as by stimulating the religious consciousness. It was assisted by the low material level of life in the centuries following the break-up of the Roman Empire. When men have no hope of improving their material condition they are more likely to believe in the power of the spirit to transfigure, if not to transform, those conditions. The medieval culture exhibited, as perhaps no other ever has, a combination of high spiritual and intellectual development with material squalor. But the tension could not last, and the centrifugal forces were too strong. When man broke out into the modern world he was set on a course that led to idolatry and atheism, notwithstanding the effort of Protestantism to recall man as an unfettered individual to those responsibilities before God which he had repudiated when he broke loose from the fold of the medieval Church.

But the Promethean revolt of modern man is not the whole story. "Now is the judgment of this world: now shall the prince of this world be cast out. And I, if I be lifted up from the earth, will draw all men unto myself."* The world cannot escape the challenge of the Cross before which even the devils tremble. Philosophical propositions may be disputed, ethical teaching may be rejected, but no selfishness or greed for wealth or power in the beholder can change the goodness of Christ into anything but goodness. And He has His continued witnesses in the saints and martyrs of Christian history. Wherever the Gospel has been preached, evil can never again claim the protection of the darkness of primitive moral ignorance, but must be for ever haunted by its own creeping shadow cast by the light from which it cannot escape.

Meanwhile Christian charity works like leaven within human systems based on expediency and self-interest, making them less selfish and less ruthless than they would otherwise be. But for the continual redemption of human systems from within by spontaneous unselfishness, civilization would long ago have failed upon the earth.† As it is, civilization exhibits two paradoxes. One is the redemption of systems based on self-interest by spontaneous unselfishness, together with the corruption, by selfishness, of systems designed for the general good. The other is the ever-increasing potential which is accumulated in the modern world both for good and for evil.

If the Cross is the key to the meaning of history, why is Christ Crucified a stumbling-block to the Jews and foolishness to the Greeks? The Jews represent all revolutionists (or, to use A. J. Toynbee's term, futurists) who seek to force the fulfilment of aspirations within history, even as Jesus' contemporaries could not understand a defeated Messiah, but expected one who would drive out the Romans and restore the Kingdom to Israel.‡ The

* John, xii. 31–32.
† There is a fuller consideration of this theme of redemption from within in a later section of this chapter (see pp. 137–140).
‡ "The Crucifixion is as great a stumbling-block in the way of futurism because the death on the Cross confirms the saying of Jesus that His kingdom is not of this World. The sign which the futurist requires is the announcement of a Kingdom which will be bereft of all meaning if it is not to be a mundane success." A. J. Toynbee: *A Study of History*, Abridged Edition, p. 529.

Greeks represent belief in human Reason, either as the philosophic detachment and tranquillity which cannot understand a suffering God, or as the self-sufficient inventiveness of man which recognizes no need of God.

Antichrist

The Christian interpretation of history, by exhibiting man's self-apotheosis and its consequences, accounts for the modern world's rejection of religion. This rejection takes two forms, one negative and agnostic, and the other positive and idolatrous.

The negative reaction has its source in that faith in man and human achievement which marked the Renaissance. For three centuries the adventure of man in the fields of science, manufacture, and commerce, carried him from wonder to wonder and triumph to triumph. Until a hundred years ago western man was still optimistic about himself and human society; he believed in progress and assumed that if everyone pursued his own self-interest the result would be the welfare of all. But, as the direction in which western civilization was moving became increasingly dubious, and man's tremendous scientific and technological achievements appeared to hold more promise of disaster than of progress, man's faith in man was shaken. "Under the perpetual smile of modernity there is a grimace of disillusion and cynicism."[*] There was less and less religion to fall back upon. And, as belief withered, the attempt to maintain the Christian ethic without the Christian religion carried less and less conviction; for there is no answer on merely ethical grounds to those who do not like the Christian ethic, no ultimate rescue from the quagmire of "Your guess is as good as mine." Meanwhile, as social and industrial processes became more technical and larger in scale, man became more and more mechanized. "Man, desiring no longer to be the image of God, becomes the image of the machine."[†] Not only has man been mechanized; he has also been bestialized. Whether mechanized or bestialized,

---

[*] Reinhold Niebuhr: *The Nature and Destiny of Man*, Vol. I, p. 129.
[†] Berdyaev: *The Fate of Man in the Modern World*, p. 26.

man is depersonalized. This is the tragic and ironic result of the humanist forces released at the Renaissance; the last four hundred years have witnessed not the completion but the reversal of the process which, through Hebrew religion, Greek life and thought, and the experience of the Christian Church, had built up the idea of man as a person. No wonder that the humanist tradition, with its faith in truth, beauty, and goodness and in the dignity of man, is discredited. No wonder that man recoils from the demonic depths of his own nature, disclosed by psychological analysis or released by political experiments. Yet even the new pessimism has not destroyed man's belief that human ingenuity and invention can somehow extricate civilization from the mess, if only the right devices or techniques can be found. This belief is no longer sanguine. It is desperate. And it persists not because there is any evidence to support it but because there is nothing beneath it but despair.

The bankruptcy of humanism is something which Christians cannot view with equanimity. It would be a great mistake for Christians to cold-shoulder humanism because it is less than Christian. Christians are bound to think that humanism is not enough—or, rather, that the true humanism is that which is taken up into a Christian synthesis. But to say this is to recognize that humanism is one part of Christian truth. That man is made in God's image is as true as that man is a fallen creature, and disregard of the first proposition throws the whole picture as badly out of perspective as disregard of the second. It is true that "western humanism springs from religious and 'transcendental' sources, without which it would be incomprehensible even to itself."* But, as Maritain also says: ". . . it is impossible to sever the tradition of humanism from the great wisdom of the pagans,"† and the great pagans, with their essential humility and natural piety, came near to the Kingdom of God. "Humanism . . . essentially tends to render man more truly human and to make his original greatness manifest by causing him to participate in all that can enrich him in nature and history. . . . Thus

* Jacques Maritain: *True Humanism*, p. xiv.
† *Ibid.*, p. xii.

understood, humanism is inseparable from civilization and culture. . . ."*

". . . St. Francis understood that, before being exploited by our industry to our use, material nature demands in some way to be itself familiarized by our Love: I mean that in loving things and the being in them man should rather draw things up to the human level than reduce humanity to their measure."† It is in the modern reversal of values, by which the material has come to be the measure of the spiritual, and the spiritual is thought of as a kind of fluorescence on the surface of the material, that humanism has lost its nerve. Every effort should be made to help humanism to recover its morale—to recover its belief in Truth, Beauty, and Goodness as transcendental values, recognized but not constituted by the mind of man, and its belief in the human soul as sacred. Although Christians cannot be satisfied with a humanism that is not a Christian humanism, they must recognize that the faith of Socrates and Plato is a great potential ally against contemporary idolatry, and shares this with Christianity, that, while it respects human dignity, it does not worship man. It is when he worships himself that man is least truly himself.

If the negative reaction against religion is a degeneration of humanism into an ineffective agnosticism, the positive reaction takes the idolatrous form of some kind of totalitarianism, in which the state, the mass, the class, or the party, is set up as god. Unreserved submission to a human collective may offer security and some measure of social justice (that, in fact, is its appeal); but the consequence of such idolatry is the denial of personality and the destruction of personal values. When party or class or

* *Ibid.* Compare the temper of these words of Simmias' in the *Phaedo*. "I feel myself how hard, or rather impossible, is the attainment of any certainty about questions such as these in the present life. And yet I should deem him a coward who did not prove what is said about them to the uttermost, or whose heart failed him before he had examined them on every side. For he should persevere until he has achieved one of two things; either he should discover or be taught the truth about them; or if this be impossible I would have him take the best and most irrefragable of human theories and let this be the raft upon which he sails through life—not without risk, as I admit, if he cannot find some word of God which will more surely and safely carry him."

† *Ibid.*, p. xv.

state is supreme, love, pity, and mercy lose their claim. Anything may be done to a liquidated class; the liquidated have no rights.

In accord with the denial of the personal is that *externalization* of history and the social process which has been noticed before* and on which Berdyaev makes the comment that man has been "stripped of soul."† Preoccupation with processes rather than with persons leads to a habit of thinking of social change in terms of trends rather than in terms of responsibility. Depersonalized thinking is too often a reflection of depersonalized living, and the great danger is that absorption in huge collectives may destroy the essential meaning of human life.

When totalitarianism comes into collision with a liberalism enfeebled by doubts, totalitarianism is likely to have the best of the encounter, to begin with at all events. The positive reaction is more effective than the negative reaction, idolatry is more vigorous than agnosticism, perversion than denial.

It is important to recognize that the modern reaction against religion—in its negative and positive forms, non-religion and anti-religion—has been let loose by Christianity itself and would have been impossible without it. It was Christianity which gave human personality the value which, in the Renaissance assertion of the unfettered individual, released the full creativeness of man. The legend of the Grand Inquisitor in Dostoevski's *The Brothers Karamazov* is true, in that the evils of the world come from Christ's terrible gift of freedom. Christianity has raised sin to a higher power by liberating man.‡ It is this fact which explains why the anti-Christian forces in the modern world are so mixed up with the Christian tradition—why essentially Christian principles such as the equality of rights which derives from a common humanity are professed and fought for by people who

---

* The change from belief in the transformation of systems from within by the human spirit to belief in the transformation of man from the outside by the manipulation of systems.

† *The Meaning of History*, p. 9.

‡ "The revolt against Christianity in the nineteenth and twentieth centuries was based upon the active principles implicit in Christianity." Berdyaev: *The Meaning of History*, p. 36.

reject Christian belief, and equally why the Christian bodies often fail to stand unequivocally for the practical implications of their doctrine. Dr. A. J. Toynbee has this to say about the historical derivation of Marxism: ". . . the elements that have made communism an explosive force are not of Hegel's creation; they bear on their face their certificate of origin from the ancestral religious faith of the west—a Christianity which, three hundred years after the philosophic challenge from Descartes, was still being drunk in by every Western child with its mother's milk and imbibed by every Western man and woman in the air they breathed. And such elements as cannot be traced to Christianity can be traced to Judaism, the 'fossilized' parent of Christianity. . . . Marx has taken a goddess 'Historical Necessity' in place of Jahweh for his deity, and the internal proletariat of the Western World in place of Jewry for his chosen people, and his Messianic Kingdom is conceived of as a Dictatorship of the Proletariat; but the salient features of the Jewish Apocalypse protrude through this threadbare disguise."* In whatever form he appears, Antichrist is dependent upon Christ and has no meaning without Him. This is no reason for complacency among Christians; quite the reverse, for Antichrist arises out of the failure of Christians and his appearance is a judgment on the Christian Church.

Modes of Redemption

Although the full meaning of history and the full redemption of mankind lie beyond this world, the redemptive power of love is active all the time in the world. The real "struggle" throughout history is not the class struggle but the struggle between the forces of good and evil, and this struggle goes on in individuals, in social groups, and in civilization as a whole. Our view of the nature of history is incomplete without some examination of the modes of redemption. The key to this question can be found in two apparently contradictory sayings of Jesus. One is: "My Kingdom is not

* *A Study of History* (Abridged Edition), pp. 399–400.

of this world."* The other is: "The Kingdom of God is within you."†

In all ages there are some—the saints and martyrs—called to witness to the truth by the sacrifice of everything, perhaps of life itself. By the refusal to compromise and the consequent acceptance of utter defeat at the hands of this world, the martyr has an *ultimate* effect on history greater than could be achieved by any direct impact on events. This is the power of the "Kingdom of God which is not in time . . . but in a different spiritual dimension," and which A. J. Toynbee says "just by virtue of this difference of dimension is able to penetrate our mundane life and transfigure it."‡

The other and more normal mode of redemption is that of the kingdom "within"—the leaven of Christian charity§ working to transform systems from within. Wherever there are some who play the game better than the rules, there is a possibility of improving the rules. The state would not have provided the present economic protection and educational facilities for young people without the philanthropic work of enlightened employers from Robert Owen to George Cadbury and educators from Hannah More to Rachel MacMillan.

* John xviii. 36. Dr. Moffatt's version is: "My realm does not belong to this world; if my realm did belong to this world my men would have fought. . . ." Mgr. Knox has: "My Kingdom, said Jesus, does not belong to this world . . . my kingdom does not take its origin here." In any case the contrast is between worldly power and the true authority of the spirit.

† Luke xvii. 21. Moffatt has: "The reign of God is now in your midst," and Knox: "The Kingdom of God is here, within you." Whether the translation is "within" or "among," the meaning seems to be that the Kingdom is already present as a spiritual principle working like leaven in men's hearts.

‡ *Vide Supra*, p. 128. In his discussion of historical responses, Toynbee contrasts Archaism and Futurism with Detachment and Transfiguration. Archaism and Futurism both try to "break away from an irksome present by taking a flying leap out of it into another reach of time without abandoning the plane of mundane life on earth." (Abridged Edition, p. 515.) Both reactions tend to be violent and fail, though there may be temporary success by futuristic devices in the political field. Nazism is an example of archaism; Jewish Messianism and Marxism are examples of futurism. Detachment and transfiguration are spiritualizations of archaism and futurism. Detachment is mystical abstraction. Transfiguration is "withdrawal and return." Both represent a "genuine change in spiritual clime and not a mere transfer in the time dimension." (*Ibid.*, p. 438.)

§ The use of the term is not meant to deny that truly Christian charity is shown by many who are not professing Christians, and that many Christians are lacking in charity.

We are so much in the habit of taking self-interest (of individuals and groups) for granted as the prevailing motive in human affairs that we tend to underestimate the importance of unselfishness as a factor in history. Although motives are seldom unmixed, a political or economic organization cannot work smoothly, or even work at all for long, without a good measure of generosity among the people concerned. The basis of any stable and contented community is goodwill, and goodwill means the readiness to give a little more than one must, without too closely counting the cost, and to take a little less than one's due. This spirit is found throughout a nation, in neighbourly kindness among millions of homes, in public service often freely given, abundantly in professions such as medicine and teaching, and in industry and commerce. We are so accustomed to think of employers and employed as natural enemies that it is easy to forget that industry can only work at all so long as there is some sense of partnership between all concerned. When sectional interests outweigh other considerations, the system cannot continue.

Many examples can be found of reforms (such as factory legislation and the spread of education) which have begun with voluntary humanitarian effort, building up enough public opinion to bring the state into action with its much greater financial resources. And the thesis could be maintained that those communities develop most happily and healthily in which social change proceeds from an awakened social conscience rather than is forced upon a selfish but enfeebled governing class. The skein of history is tangled. It is true that benefactors may change their attitude towards the recipients of their generosity when they realize the full consequences of their actions.* And it is also true that most of the violent assaults on privilege would have been impossible without previous concessions which enabled the unprivileged to become articulate and effective. But confused as the picture is, the active leaven of unselfishness and charity is as real a factor in history as the corruption of all human systems.

* Victorian radicals would have been horrified to see the world of to-day which they helped to create.

And the duty of Christians is clearly to work for the redemption of social systems by increasing the potential of goodwill in the community. To what extent the objective should be to make the existing system work as well as possible, or to change the system, is a question that can be answered only in relation to circumstances. And to some extent the alternative is unreal; for there is truth in the paradox that to make the best of a system is to change it.* In any case it is people that make systems and not systems that make people.

Christians and the Social Order

The key to true community is to be found in the meaning of the personal. "A great and full relation between man and man can only exist between unified and responsible persons. That is why it is much more rarely found in the totalitarian collective than in any historically earlier form of society; much more rarely also in the authoritarian party than in any earlier form of association. Genuine education for character is genuine education for community."† Another way of expressing this truth is in terms of A. J. Toynbee's thesis that "the transference of the field of action from the macrocosm to the microcosm" is the criterion of the growth of civilization.‡ That is to say, the true development is towards inwardness rather than outwardness. What matters most is, as Edward Wilson put it, not circumstances but the spirit in which people respond to circumstances. The greatest effects of Christianity in history are indirect rather than direct, by the remaking of people rather than the manipulation of external events—by the victory over evil in the soul. This is

* There is possibly a cleavage of ethical principle here between the Christian attitude and that of the secular revolutionary who deliberately seeks to discredit and sabotage a system in the hope of expediting its collapse.

† Martin Buber: *Between Man and Man*, p. 116. An authoritarian party does not develop responsible persons so much as provide an escape from personal responsibility. Response to situations tends to be according to predetermined norms, whereas the true personal response is made as though *ab initio*.

‡ *A Study of History* (Abridged Edition), p. 438. Of "futurism" Dr. Toynbee says (p. 431): ". . . the effort to live in the microcosm instead of the macrocosm is abandoned for the pursuit of a Utopia, which would be reached—supposing it could actually be found in real life—without any challenge to face the arduous change of spiritual clime."

what A. J. Toynbee means by "transfiguration" and the "transference of the field of action from the macrocosm to the microcosm." There must in a sense be a withdrawal from the process of history into the soul, which, by taking the world's evil into the soul, defeats it there. From that victory new creative power flows back into the historical process. And, since no ideal can be fully achieved in the world, but always encounters some measure of defeat, there must perpetually be this withdrawal into the soul, in order to defeat there the evil that cannot be overcome on the mundane level. Here is another most important aspect of the truth that Christ reveals the nature of history; for this victory in the soul which overcomes worldly defeat and returns with new power into the process of history is nothing less than Crucifixion as a historical principle. Many illustrations can be found, such as the Wesleyan movement, of a power to turn the world upside down which depends upon a certain abdication from the world and a creation of the Kingdom within. But— and this is important—there can never be final abdication; the significance of the withdrawal is *reculer pour mieux sauter*.

The creation of personal quality is the means by which systems can be transformed from within. The wrong development is the externalization of life, which has been going on in the modern world, accompanied by the devaluation of the personal and the illusion that man can be transformed from without.

It follows that the Christian attitude to social change must be one that respects personality and therefore must reject "futurism" and all other attitudes which in the last resort subordinate persons to systems. Christian charity must include the liquidated in mercy and must realize that all change for the better involves the destruction of some real values—and must be sensitive to the values destroyed as well as to new values created. The Christian attitude will therefore be in sympathy with persuasion as the instrument of change, with organic growth as the mode of change, and with the greatest freedom for variety within unity as the type of society to be aimed at.

Although Christians must put persons before systems, it would be a great mistake to think that Christianity is "other-worldly" in the sense of recognizing no obligations in respect of the social order. There is a good deal of confusion on this matter. Christians are sometimes challenged on the ground that, as Christians, they ought to identify themselves with a particular political programme. Such a challenge is beside the point.* Christianity neither identifies itself with political programmes nor condemns political programmes *per se*. Christianity affirms certain enduring values, and leaves to each generation the task of interpreting those values in the changing idiom of historical development. Christianity condemns, not this or that system, but the sinfulness of man which corrupts all systems. This does not mean, however, that political and economic systems are a matter of indifference to Christians. Christians, together with everyone else, must recognize that in the process of history some systems become impossible to maintain and give place to others. But, while historical change certainly alters the form in which man's eternal problems present themselves, there is no evidence that it solves those problems. It may solve some while creating others; for example, the problem of how to find security in an individualistic society may give place to the problem of how to find freedom in a collectivist society.

The Christian attitude towards systems, put very simply, is this. Theoretically, any system could provide the context of the perfect community, given enough goodwill. In practice some systems are, in given circumstances, more conducive to the good life than others; and Christians, like other people, ought to make their own political decisions; the failure to do so is less pardonable in Christians than in others. No system, however, in any circumstances, carries a guarantee of human perfection, since the character of a system in operation depends on the quality of the persons operating it. No system is a guarantee against selfishness, greed, and suspicion. One system may make economic exploitation impossible, but there is plenty of evidence that men, denied one means of exploiting their fellows, will find others. Christians therefore must think of social progress, not in terms of arriving at the right stage of historical development,

* E.g. Mr. Gallacher's letter to *The Times*, 17th November, 1948.

but in terms of the potential of goodwill available in the community for making the best of the existing system and thereby changing it. But to recognize a necessary and reciprocal relationship between persons and systems is quite a different thing from believing that a particular system contains any guarantee in itself for good or evil.

Christianity, then, cannot identify itself with political programmes, though Christians have their political responsibilities which ought to involve them as individuals in political loyalties. The fact that the Christian faith does not carry a political "directive" puts the Christian Church at an obvious disadvantage *vis-à-vis* a creed which subordinates everything to the fulfilment of a programme. And the Christian obligation to put eternal values before worldly objectives means that, for Christians, a political issue can never be as clear as it is to those who conceive their goal in worldly terms alone. It is in the nature of Christianity that the worldly programme is never an end in itself. Christians therefore can never say: "The programme shall be driven through, come what may; and no considerations of mercy or pity or veneration shall hinder it." The strength of a creed like Marxian Communism is precisely that it can quite consistently say: "Nothing shall stand in the way of the programme." For Christians a situation may arise when to proceed at all costs with the programme is to compromise the ultimate values of human personality and freedom. This does not mean that Christians must never use any weapon but reasoned persuasion, for no human society could be maintained at all on those terms alone. It means that there are occasions in which the only possible choice is a choice of evils. To fight evil with its own weapons is always dangerous, for we tend to become more like the thing we are fighting against and less like the thing we are fighting for. The fight for social justice may easily degenerate into a mobilization of the selfishness of the poor against the selfishness of the rich. But if we refuse in all circumstances to soil our hands with violence we fail to recognize that, as members of human society, we stand committed to its imperfections and to the expedients to which it may be necessary to resort in emergency. No doubt a Hitler ought not to be allowed to get into power, and possibly he could have been prevented by peaceful means. But that is not an argument for letting him overrun Europe.

From this dilemma there is no escape. The Christian lives both in the world and beyond the world. He is involved in all the imperfection of the world and can never disentangle himself from the implications of the world's evil. Yet, equally, he must suffer continual crucifixion at the hands of the world and must try to transform defeat into victory by carrying the struggle inward into the soul. And there is nothing to be gained by not squarely recognizing the embarrassments involved in the attempt to live the Christian life. Yet another embarrassment arises from the sins of omission and commission of which historical Christianity is guilty. However much Christians may deplore the atheism of Marxian Communism (and Marxism is the first large-scale and explicit onslaught on Christianity), the fact remains that Marxism arose as a passionate protest against social injustice. Christians must come under this condemnation and recognize in the Marxist attack a judgment of history on the failure of Christian civilization which has a shameful record in the matter of social justice.

It is worth observing that Christianity is the only salvationist religion which is world-affirming and not world-negating—that is to say, which takes this world seriously as the proper field of spiritual activity. This is the reason why Christianity is so full of tension and difficulty—and also so full of meaning. The dilemma can be escaped by a creed for which this world is nothing (such as Buddhism) as completely as by a creed for which the world is everything. Christianity can no more disregard political and economic problems than it can disregard problems of personal conduct. In fact the distinction is a false one. Christianity is as much concerned about democracy as about monogamy, and for *the same reasons*—that is, because certain institutions, in certain circumstances, are or are not conducive to right relations of persons. Christianity is therefore very much concerned to point out and present to the contemplation of mankind certain forms of social relationship, which we may broadly call democratic, as being, under modern conditions, more conducive than others to a true valuation and exercise of personal life. And to imagine that Christianity is only concerned with social relations to the extent of exhorting people to forbearance and kindliness is a great mistake. But this essential connection between Christianity and democracy is nevertheless a quite different thing from the identification of Christianity with a social or political programme. The difference is that Christianity always recognizes that the Kingdom of Heaven can break into being in the context of *any* social order and that no social order can be a guarantee of the Kingdom of Heaven on earth. The matter is well put in this passage from Archbishop Temple's *Christianity and Social Order*: "The method of the Church's impact upon society at large should be twofold. The Church must announce Christian principles and point out where the existing social order at any time is in conflict with them. It must then pass on to Christian citizens, acting in their civic capacity, the task of re-shaping the existing order in closer conformity to the principles. For at this point technical knowledge may be required and judgments of practical expediency are always required. . . . The Church may tell the politician what ends the social order should promote; but it must leave to the politician the devising of the precise means to these ends. This is a point of first-rate importance, and is frequently misunderstood. If Christianity is true at all it is a truth of universal application; all things should be done in the Christian spirit and in accordance with Christian principles. 'Then', say some, 'produce your Christian solution of unemployment.' But there neither is nor can be such a thing. . . . 'In that case', says the reformer—or, quite equally, the upholder of the *status quo*— 'keep off the turf. By your own confession you are out of place here.' But this time the Church must say: 'No; I cannot tell you what is the remedy; but I can tell you that a society of which unemployment (in peace time) is a chronic feature is a diseased society, and that if you are not doing all you can to find and administer the remedy, you are guilty before God.' Sometimes the Church can go farther than this and point to features in the social structure itself which are bound to be sources of social evil because they contradict the principles of the Gospel."*

* *Christianity and Social Order*, pp. 35–6.

IX
The Christian Teacher

ALONE of the great religious insights the Hebrew-Christian tradition stands for a dynamic view of history, as revealing the nature and destiny of man, and therefore fully accepts the life of the world as a proper field for spiritual effort. No other religion could have maintained the same vital historical relation with a civilization marked as no other civilization has been by profound and accelerating social change. At the same time, the Hebrew-Christian affirmation of the sacredness of human personality—a sacredness that belongs to man because man belongs to eternity as well as to time—is the necessary ultimate justification of a belief in democracy and the basis of the rights of man. The other great religions are not interested in democracy nor in social development. It is because of its unique concern about both these things that Christianity is also by its nature interested in education.

Christianity, Democracy, and Education

A rapidly changing, technological civilization is necessarily democratic in the sense that its technical developments make it increasingly necessary for the people at large to assume intelligent responsibility—the alternative being a very unstable kind of slave state in which the slaves have to know too much to be safe. Western civilization is therefore interested, as no other civilization has been, in the education of the people at large. Other civilizations may have been interested in the professional education of a ruling class or the polite education of a leisured class, but not in the education of the whole community as responsible citizens.

Earlier in this book it was argued that the supreme challenge to education in our generation is to be found in the need for freedom in community. It is worth remembering that both freedom and community are essential to the Christian meaning of personal life. Christian belief and Christian obedience are not blind. Personal responsibility for thought and action remain a Christian duty, and the claim of Christianity is never one that takes from us the obligation to be the authors of our own response. Christ never takes from us our power to reject Him. As to community, redemption is always redemption into a society—an *ecclesia*. The Bible knows nothing of the redemption of individuals *in vacuo*, but the Bible is full of pictures of social redemption—the "Kingdom of Heaven," "where two or three are gathered together," "the Communion of Saints."

The necessary concern of Christianity about education has its foundations in the Christian belief about man and about history. Since Christianity takes history seriously, man must be as well equipped as possible for playing his part in it. The whole of man's nature, body and mind, must be fully developed. Christianity gives no sanction to a view of education in which the spiritual faculties alone are cultivated and the body and the senses neglected. It is true that Christian education must have a single focus; everything must be done *Ad Majorem Dei Gloriam*; but this is quite a different thing from a lopsided development of human beings.*

In Christian belief man's worth arises, not from his civic status, but from his being a child of God. Because children of God, all men are brothers. Herein is the ground of the doctrine of the equality of all men and of the interest of Christianity in universal education. The Christian pressure towards education and democracy can be seen throughout history. But the picture is complicated by the fact that Christianity cannot by any means be fully identified with the historical Churches. The Church, as a human organization, is susceptible to the corruption of power, has often become authoritarian and dogmatic, and has used its influence to maintain vested interests. Thus the situation has certain paradoxical features. Organized Churches have been found on the side of privileged authority and against democracy

---

* Neoplatonic influence in the Christian Church is responsible for a contempt (or despair) of the world and the body; but there is no authority for this attitude in the New Testament.

and universal education. Social and educational aims which have their origin in Christian thought and experience are promoted by secular agencies which repudiate religious authority and even deny religious truth; Christian individuals and groups, often dissenting from the established Churches, again and again show initiative in the cause of democracy and education.

The Church saved civilization when the Roman Empire collapsed, and sustained it through the Middle Ages, maintaining intellectual life through the education of the clerk and civilizing barbarism through the education of the knight. The Thomist synthesis of Christianity and Greek philosophy made it possible for the humanism of the Renaissance to be prepared under the cloak of orthodoxy. The secular gusto of the southern Renaissance expressed itself in the education of the courtier. In the north, education retained a more religious and democratic aim. Luther's "Every man a priest" was full of import for democratic education in the long run. The principle that every man must learn to read, in order to understand the Bible for himself, is the most important contribution of the Reformation to education, and some German principalities made education compulsory on the strength of it.

But, if the Church of the Middle Ages gave way to the corruption of empire, the Churches of the Reformation yielded to the corruption of nationalism and commercial enterprise, and to that extent were weakened as agents of education. More and more education passed into secular hands. Speculation and experiment were conducted in secular terms and on secular assumptions, from Condorcet's belief in the "indefinite perfectibility of man" to the psychology of Thorndyke.

The promotion of democracy and universal education has thus been largely the work of secular agencies, and the modern world has presented the paradoxical spectacle of the Church acting against the nature of Christianity and secular or even anti-religious organizations promoting Christian ideals.

At the same time the initiative of religious groups has been an important factor in the spread of education, especially among the poor. Such enterprise in England is illustrated by the

Dissenting Academies of the seventeenth and eighteenth centuries, the Wesleyan movement, and—when the advance of industrialization was making both literacy and social education positively necessary—the Sunday Schools and the monitorial schools. For three-quarters of the nineteenth century, virtually the whole burden of popular education was borne by religious bodies. And throughout the century, although the established church was on the whole opposed to the intervention of the State in education and to that extent tended to hamper the spread of education in the latter part of the century, the devoted work of countless parish clergy, often making up deficiencies out of their own pockets, was a factor of first-rate importance in building up English elementary education.

Since the Churches are human organizations, subject to human failings, it is not surprising (least of all is it surprising to Christians themselves) that the Churches have often promoted other things on earth than the Kingdom of Heaven. The educational work of the Church of England during the last two hundred years is an interesting story of conflicting tendencies—piety, philanthropy, self-sacrifice, snobbery, suspicion, bigotry, and inertia. The non-conformist bodies have not been hindered by a traditional association with privilege and the *status quo*, but they have lacked money and power. The Roman Catholics have been most uncompromising in their maintenance of the principle of the denominational school, but their object has perhaps been to spread Catholicism rather than to improve education. It cannot be said that any of the Churches has really made any great and imaginative effort to show the world what a modern Christian school should be (or a Christian college for that matter). The reason for this weakness is not far to seek and is surely to be found in the failure of institutional Christianity to cope with the modern world in general—to assimilate science and industrialism and consequent social change, and to reinterpret the Christian gospel in terms of our own world. Moreover, among many of the well-intentioned, there is a good deal of misunderstanding as to what re-interpretation means. It does not mean paring down the Gospel to something less than the

Gospel by making concessions to scientists and politicians. It does mean expressing the whole Gospel in the idiom and through the experience of our own world, and thereby enriching it—as the Fourth Gospel enriched the truth of the Incarnation by re-interpreting it in terms of the *Logos*.*

The Christian teacher, then, must reckon with the weakness of the Churches, and must realize that the Churches need a large measure of re-education to make them effective instruments of the Gospel in society. It is at least encouraging that the Churches themselves are aware of this need, and are showing a new interest in education. At the same time there has been a swing of official lay opinion towards a positive appreciation of the value of religion in education. It is a far cry from the Elementary Code of 1904, in which the aims of education were stated in purely ethical terms without any reference to religion, to the Act of 1944, which requires an act of worship each day in the school. The change, though largely pragmatic in its motives, is none the less significant of an uneasiness lest a purely secular education should prove unequal to the demands of modern life.

Whatever may be the shortcomings of the Churches, Christian teachers must remember that Christianity without Churches is bound to be a precarious and incomplete thing. The organized religious community—the *ecclesia*—is essential to the full Christian life. The New Testament knows nothing of religion as a private affair between a man and his God. Christianity has always meant reception into a community. And religious education in schools, so far from disregarding the Churches, ought to help to pass on the boys and girls into adult church membership.

Christian Belief and Modern Educational Theory

It is sometimes assumed that orthodox Christian belief is incompatible with the findings of modern psychology. To this attitude it is hardly sufficient to reply: "So much the worse for modern psychology!" for psychologists quite rightly take their work

---

* The Fourth Gospel reminds us that re-interpretation not only enriches the thing interpreted but also transforms the idiom in which it is re-interpreted.

seriously. It is worth pointing out, however, that there are many good psychologists who are Christians, and that their psychology and their Christianity lose nothing, but rather gain, from the combination. The truth is that modern systematic study of the human mind, and particularly the exploration of its hidden emotional depths, has confirmed rather than exploded the Christian doctrine of man. What modern psychology helps to explode is something quite different—namely, the irreligious assumption of human self-perfectibility to which many modern psychologists obstinately cling, not because they are psychologists but because, as moderns, they are infected with the spirit of the age.

In an earlier chapter some attention was paid to the habit among some psychologists of confusing sin and guilt. Guilt is a morbid symptom, but sin is a fact of man's nature and the sense of sin is a humble and healthy recognition of that fact. Guilt arises from a refusal to face facts and a desire not to be found out. · The distinction between sin and guilt is perfectly clear to those who are not bemused by the illusion of human self-sufficiency. It is only when man is thought of as self-perfectible and the need for salvation by divine grace is denied, that it becomes necessary to deny also the fact of sin and the propriety of a sense of sin. The confusion between sin and guilt is a simple way of doing this, for it enables sin to be drawn into the same condemnation as guilt.

It is most important to recognize that the modern dogma of human self-sufficiency receives no endorsement whatever from modern psychology, but is itself material for psychological diagnosis inasmuch as it is an example of wishful thinking on the part of modern man who has nothing left to believe in. On the contrary, the cumulative effect of modern psychology, with its alarming disclosure of the demonic depths of the human psyche, is to strike as heavy a blow against the doctrine of man as self-perfectible reason as modern history has struck against the doctrine of progress.

Hostility to the doctrine of Original Sin does not proceed legitimately from the study of psychology, but rather is a dogma superimposed upon psychological thinking. The same is true of those physiological and biological preoccupations which have characterized certain modern schools of psychology and have given plausibility to the view that psychology has discredited religion.

The worthy attempt to make psychology scientific led, especially in America, to a concentration of attention upon the physiological side of behaviour, since in this field objective observation and measurement are possible. Psychology thus became almost a branch of physiology, and the extreme doctrine of *Epiphenomenalism* represents mental events as being nothing but a kind of mirage on the surface of brain-processes. It is, of course, perfectly legitimate to define a field of investigation in any way that is thought convenient, and scientists are entitled to restrict themselves to this physiological psychology if they wish. The danger is in forgetting that there has been any restriction, and in allowing a technique of investigation to give rise to a philosophy. Scientists are extremely prone to this kind of muddled thinking, which in this instance takes the form of assuming that the human mind is nothing more than those aspects of it which happen to have been studied.

The same mistake marks the *behaviourists*, who, very properly protesting against introspective methods that were incapable of proof, proposed to limit the field of inquiry to those things (outward behaviour) which could be objectively established. The error of behaviourism consists in the assumption that, because human behaviour can be conveniently studied in terms of stimulus and response, therefore there is nothing in human behaviour except a quasi-reflex response to stimulus. It is only fair to add that many behaviourists do in fact distinguish between behaviourism as a discipline and behaviourism as a philosophy.

Against the mechanistic tendencies of the behaviourists and the epiphenomenalists the German schools (prominently that of Freud) put forward an essentially purposive view of the nature of mental activity. "Determinism" is a misleading term as applied to Freud's psychology. His school, although it "professes 'strict determinism,' is thoroughly hormic—that is to say, it recognizes that all mental activity, conscious or unconscious, is sustained by impulsions towards goals."* Freud's categories are biological rather than physiological. He is "deterministic" not in the sense that motive is thought of as *vis a tergo*, but in the sense that human behaviour is assumed to be fundamentally determined by the pleasure-pain principle. From this ultimate hedonism there is no escape, for he holds that the discipline of the super-ego leads inevitably to complexes and aberrations. In Freud's view, therefore, man is always in the dilemma of which one horn is primitive animalism and the other is mental disease.

In Freud's final pessimism we have another, and very interesting, example of a preconceived doctrine superimposed upon a system of psychology. Freud's attempt to reduce the complexities of the human spirit to biological terms "fails to explain how biological impulses should have been transmuted into such highly complex spiritual phenomena."† That is to say, either we must suppose that animals suffer from Oedipus complexes and the like, or else we must conclude that the human spirit cannot be thus reduced to biological terms. What Freud's thought really demonstrates is the inadequacy of a "naturalistic" interpretation of man; and the final impasse in which it ends is at least presumptive evidence against his "debunking" of religion.

In all these examples of types of psychology, the same fallacy appears: namely the assumption that, because a certain part of the whole field is selected for observation, therefore it is the whole field. As an interesting and important reaction against this disintegrative tendency it is worth mentioning the Gestalt school with its emphasis on the totality of behaviour and its interest in restoring the whole person, only comprehensible as a whole, as the proper object of study.

Modern psychology has certainly revealed nothing that contradicts Christian doctrine. What is surprising (or what would be surprising if modern psychology had not familiarized

---

* W. McDougall: *Modern Materialism and Emergent Evolution*, p. 217.
† Reinhold Niebuhr: *The Nature and Destiny of Man*, Vol. I, p. 45.

us with the contrariness of the human mind) is the obstinacy with which some psychologists cling to a doctrine of man for which their science supplies not a shred of evidence.

In a sense, of course, there is nothing new in modern psychology. Modern child study has not established new truths but has thrown fresh light on old truths in such a way as to leave us no excuse for disregarding them. The central revelation of modern child study is the oldest truth of all about education—that the first and last principle of education is love; that is to say, we must respect the personality of the child and treat him as an end in himself and secure his *present* needs. We must never exploit our power and influence over the child to secure *our* convenience. Above all the child needs love and security. Therefore we must not let him feel that the love he needs has to be won by placating us. Conversely, he must not discover that he can get power over adults by annoying them.*

But the modern emphasis on the child's need of security, freedom, and activity, does not justify the belief that the child is "naturally good" in the sense that if left to develop "naturally" it will be perfectly satisfactory. The conflict in man is within him, not between him and the environment, and cannot be solved at the level of adjustment to the environment. Modern psychology has not disposed of original sin.

No view of education is adequate which does not reckon with spiritual conflict as man's peculiar heritage. Man's supreme problem is to find reconciliation through and beyond the conflict. The long and painful journey begins even in the cradle and ends beyond the grave. The wrestling with the conflict is not an easy business, however favourable the environment. Nor must we expect too much assistance from the environment. Every environment has its own characteristic pitfalls. Human life cannot be made easy, nor growth painless. There is no education without tears†—or, if there is, it fails utterly to reach

* The literature of war-time evacuation is full of evidence of children's need of love and security. And it has become almost a commonplace that a home must be very bad indeed to be worse than no home at all.

† That is no justification for thinking that there is any virtue in making the tears flow.

the full dimensions of human life and will bring its own retribution. We must educate for the Kingdom of Heaven, nothing less. And this means submitting ourselves to be judged by God's standards, not judging God by our standards. The Kingdom of Heaven is not the Garden of Eden, nor is it "citizenship," nor "social adjustment," nor the "development of individual potentiality." But it is something which, if sought first, will bring all these things with it.

The Paradox of Christian Loyalty

It was urged in an earlier chapter that Christians ought not to withhold co-operation with secular humanists because they are less than Christian. Elsewhere emphasis has been laid on the ultimate cleavage between the Christian view of man as a fallen child of God and the noblest pagan view of man as a rational animal. That cleavage is real and, because of it, Christians find themselves in a dilemma as to how they should co-operate with enlightened humanists who are not professing Christians. If they insist on the fundamental cleavage, they cause division and may destroy a valuable basis of practical co-operation; they seem to bring not peace but a sword. If they soft-pedal their differences of ultimate belief they may betray the things that are most important of all by tacitly consenting to the assumption that the only difference between Christian and secular belief is one of picturesque language, in which "God" is a name for ultimate reality, "sin" means maladjustment, and "salvation" means natural development. The difficult and paradoxical solution of the problem is that Jesus' apparently contradictory sayings: "He that is not with me is against me" (Matt. xiii. 30) and "He that is not against us is for us" (Mk. ix. 40) are *both true*. it is possible for men of goodwill to walk together though their ways divide. The discovery and understanding of cleavages at sufficient depth is itself a form of co-operation, because it is an honest search for truth.

Wherever there are people who believe in education—that is, who give themselves to it with unselfish love, to whom their pupils' personalities are sacred, who believe that true freedom is found in right service—with all these the Christian teacher ought to co-operate positively, whole-heartedly, and humbly, recognizing that it is a privilege to join with such people in the work of the Kingdom. At the same time, no good can come (least of all to the cause of Christ) from an amiable intellectual fog about ultimate issues; and the Christian teacher must be perfectly candid about the fundamental cleavage between Christianity and secular humanism. He must do this humbly and within the bonds of charity. Nor is it easy, for the danger of being accused from without of complacency and self-righteousness is only surpassed by the danger of spiritual pride from within. When you think you have the truth and the other fellow has not, it is very hard not to feel superior. And if you can manage to avoid feeling superior and cultivate Christian humility, it is very hard not to pat yourself on the back for cultivating Christian humility. In fact the sin of pride cannot be avoided; and from this point of view the Christian is the greatest sinner of all and stands most in need of grace. The Christian who understands this paradox can do something to help the non-Christian to understand what is so often a stumbling-block—the fact that "there are so many much better people who are not Christians." The answer is that *of course* there are. It is hard to be a good man; it is impossible to be a good Christian. *Corruptio optimi pessima.* That is why, in a Christian community, there are a very few saints and a great many tiresome and rather unpleasant people.

Some Practical Implications of a Christian Philosophy of Education

The objective of Christian education can be nothing less than to win our generation to the Christian faith. Humanly speaking this is a task of enormous difficulty, since it involves the fundamental re-education of a whole civilization. We cannot set limits to the grace of God, with Whom all things are possible. But there is nothing to be gained by underestimating the difficulty of restoring Christian belief in the modern world. Some people talk as if the task were comparable with that of spreading a knowledge of dietetics or cultivating habits of cleanliness. It is often forgotten that a person is accessible only to arguments which rest upon the same fundamental assumptions as his own thinking. He must be able to establish mental contact with the message that he is invited to receive; it must have enough meaning for him to be able to agree or disagree with it. It is possible for a point of view to be so alien as to be without meaning to those to whom it is presented, because they have not the basic assumptions necessary to make it intelligible. That is in fact the position of most people to-day in relation to religious ideas. The dogma of human self-sufficiency so dominates modern thinking that the very possibility of another interpretation of man is inconceivable. Propositions about sin and redemption are empty to minds that have become incapable of thinking of man except as a rational animal improving himself by his own efforts. The language of religion has become not only metaphor but dead metaphor.

The work of re-education, therefore, must reach the level of those fundamental assumptions about man in relation to the universe on which the very possibility of religious thinking depends. That is to say, we must rediscover our sense of the reality of God's activity and of the helplessness of man when separated from God. And we must achieve this rediscovery in a cultural context that makes it more difficult than it has ever been for man to discern any reality other than man himself and the works of his own hands—which almost eliminates the kind of experience that furnishes the material of natural piety. We shall be helped in our attempt if we will remember, and use in our teaching, the truth that religious experience is not a strange and uncanny sort of experience but is normal experience understood at full depth. If we can help people to discern the religious truth implicit in everyday experience which they take for granted—the painfulness of creation, the warfare of love against its rejection, the power of love to redeem when other forces have failed—we shall have done a great deal to break down the barrier which the modern mind has erected against the light.

If the primary difficulty about religious re-education is the sheer inaccessibility of the modern mind to religious thought and feeling, the next difficulty is the prodigious ignorance of the subject* which prevails even among educated people—ignorance of Christian doctrine and, above all, of the Bible. The knowledge which we have been losing for several generations cannot be rapidly restored. It is always easier to lose knowledge than to gain it. And we have not only lost our knowledge of religion —we have even forgotten that an educated person's religion involves a great deal of knowledge, achieved by much diligent study and hard thinking. It is too easily assumed in these days that anyone has a right, without study or self-discipline, and on perfunctory consideration, to dispose of the most profound problems that have engaged the human mind. Almost worse than our lack of knowledge is this lack of standards, because it prevents us from recognizing the need for disciplined effort on our own part if we wish to understand the Christian religion. After all, one of the first principles in education should be that we have no right to an opinion in matters which we do not understand.

The religious re-education of our world is bound, humanly speaking, to be a slow and very laborious business. There can be no "return to religion" by an overnight decision under the stimulus of political or economic crisis. A return to religion which is more than disguised panic must reckon both with widespread ignorance and also with the fact that the primary assumptions of religion have become virtually unthinkable to modern man. And we have to remember, in dealing with doubt, indifference, and unbelief, that there is no "case for Christianity" in the sense that there is a "case" for, say, Free Trade. The case for Christianity is Christ, and no one can call Him Lord except by the Spirit. Conviction cannot come by intellectual processes alone; and, in the intellectual field, the considerations which

* The unbelievers have no monopoly of ignorance. There is plenty of error and confusion in the minds of professing Christians. Few can fulfil the requirement laid down by St. Peter: "being ready always to give answer to every man that asketh you a reason concerning the hope that is in you, yet with meekness and fear." 1 Peter iii. 15.

commend Christianity are such as demand prolonged study and thought.*

It is very much open to question whether we have even begun to envisage in a realistic way the task of training and equipping an effective force for religious re-education. To be properly equipped for his job the Christian teacher needs not only to acquire an adequate knowledge of the Bible and Christian doctrine, and of the principles and practice of teaching; he needs also to study the contemporary world in order to understand those movements of thought and feeling which have produced the present state of unbelief. This is a big assignment. But it is not all. For we have to recognize that active Christians, whether they are teachers or tram-drivers, have a duty to spread the Gospel in their everyday contacts with their fellows, and that for this kind of work training is as necessary as it is for a paid occupation. In other words, we need a Christian missionary army for service at home. This army would include clergy and teachers of religious knowledge in schools; but it ought also to include lay men and women, with all sorts of paid occupations, who are trained to spread the Gospel in industry or wherever they go. The mobilization of a force of such people is perhaps even more important than the training of school teachers. And the kind of training suitable for them requires careful thought and planning, and much of it would be relevant also to the needs of people, such as teachers and youth leaders, whose occupation is specifically educational.

No systematic attempt has yet been made to work out a plan for such a missionary army or for the effective co-ordination of the many agencies whose co-operation would be necessary. But it is hard to see how anything short of a comprehensive attack on the problem can have much chance of success.

And we must face the fact that a great deal of preparation of

* The chief of these considerations are perhaps the following—(a) That Christian philosophy interprets human experience, including human history, more comprehensively and at greater depth than any other philosophy; (b) that Christian theology alone affords an adequate foundation for that ethic of love which, even by secular thinkers, is acknowledged to hold the key to personal and social life; (c) Christian life and loyalty afford an eternal and unshakable spiritual security.

the ground is needed before the mind of our generation (or of the next) can become fertile soil for religious truth. Along with the religious education of those who can receive it there must be what may be called pre-religious education of the others; and this needs as much planning as direct religious instruction, or more. Educated and thoughtful sceptics must be convinced of the inadequacy of secular philosophy to do justice to the experience which needs interpretation, and shown that Christianity, so far from introducing irrelevant difficulties, offers the most complete answer to their own questions. Those who are unaware of any questions needing answers, who think of life in terms of good luck and bad luck, home, job, and the annual holiday, must be induced to see that our tiny, insulated securities are really no security—because the universe, with its depths of good and evil, suffering and love and death, not only surrounds but is within them. And all kinds of people, whether capable of thoughtful reflection or not, must be shown what concern Christianity has with social problems and also the fallacy of specious assignments for Utopia which propose to reform mankind by organization and ignore the evil in the human heart. They must be shown, too, that Christianity has standards of personal living and that Christian discipleship bears fruit in personal character, not by making saints or heroes of us all, but by taking us up, such as we are, into something greater than ourselves. The theatre provides a useful analogy here. The plays of Shakespeare not only give the great actor his supreme opportunity and his supreme test; but they also redeem the bad actor, whereas the slick plays of some modern authors only damn the bad actor.

When we survey the enormous task before us, we cannot help wondering, not only whether it is possible, but still more whether there will be time for its accomplishment before a final convulsion and catastrophe of our civilization. The forces of destruction work more quickly than the forces of construction. All we can say is that, even if we knew for certain that there could be no Kingdom of Heaven on earth (and we can never know that) we should still have an absolute obligation to strive for it. The war of the spirit may never be won in this world; but equally it is never lost.

Meanwhile, there remains the more limited problem of the contribution of the school to Christian education. In Part I it was suggested that an education designed to meet the needs of the modern world ought to contain three ingredients—(1) it should help boys and girls to understand the world they live in; (2) it should provide practical experience of living in a community; and (3) it should disclose the Vision of Greatness. It will perhaps be useful to look again at these three elements from a Christian standpoint.

A Christian study of our world will focus attention on the problem of personality (the depersonalizing and externalizing tendencies of modern civilization and the need to restore the value of the human personality), and will also reveal clearly the Christian insights into established fields of knowledge. At the heart of the school's teaching will be the Christian gospel, and this Gospel must spread its light out all through the other subjects of study. Science, for example, will be studied in reverence for God's truth, and not from an appetite to magnify human power; and it will be all the more scientific for that, because it will be more interested in truth than in exploitation. History, the projection outwards on the screen of time of man's eternal struggle with himself, will be seen to find its supreme meaning, as also its supreme judgment, in the Cross.

In practical social education the Christian school will strive to create Christian community as the context of experience for young people. The most important thing about a school (or a home, for that matter) is that it should seek to learn the Christian life and try to be an example of Christian fellowship. Any educational community trying to do that must seriously re-think some of the assumptions of traditional educational practice (e.g. the proper use of the competitive impulse, the true foundations of authority, and so on). At the heart of the school life must be worship. What form the regular acts of worship should take and where they should be held is very much a matter of opinion and circumstance. But, in any case, worship ought to be a natural and normal part of the life of the school, everything possible ought to be done to make it live, and it should help to pass on the boys and girls into adult church membership.

In presenting ideals and the lives of great people, Christian teaching will not only see that Christian thinking and living are fairly represented among the great figures of history, but will also present the Christian view of history as being essentially incarnational and as finding its norm in Christ.

In the method of its teaching the Christian school has that very difficult but not impossible task of presenting positive truths in such a way as to maintain the right and duty of those who learn to accept or reject on their own responsibility. That is to say Christian teaching must combine authority with freedom. Authority there must be. If education is to mean anything and avail anything, it must have the unity and drive that a faith strongly held alone can give. Jesus taught "as one having authority." Yet the disciple's decision must always be his own. However compelling the Christian message may be, it can never coerce. Christ never takes away our liberty to reject Him. We can point to kinds of education which claim authority but allow no freedom—where truth is subordinated to political expediency and the inculcation of orthodox opinion is more important than the power to think for oneself. And we can point to other kinds of education that give the sort of freedom which comes from lack of conviction and leads ultimately to chaos—where knowledge tends to be little more than information and the failure to present a coherent view of life is justified on the grounds that boys and girls should be left to make up their own minds—though this in fact may well mean that they are left incapable of doing so. The question is: What is the secret of the combination of authority and freedom? The answer in one word is Love. Love is the key to all true relationship between persons; in fact, persons can grow as persons only if they love and are loved. For that reason love is at the very heart of education.

Christian education therefore ends, as it begins, by laying supreme emphasis on persons. Christianity reinforces and raises to a higher power the educational aims and values to which natural reason points. That the purpose of education is to promote personal growth, and in particular to redeem the personal in a world which threatens to destroy personal values, is a conclusion that arose from an inquiry conducted without specifically religious presuppositions, as also is the recognition of love as the principle which alone can reconcile the claims of individual and community. An appeal to Christianity does not produce a *different* answer to our central problems, but gives full meaning and full authority to the answer which was already indicated. Christianity shows us *why* the human soul is sacred, and why man cannot perfect himself; it explains the strange tension between the things of this world and the things of eternity; and it makes sense of the enigma of life out of death, victory in defeat, the power of the weak things to confound the things that are mighty. The Christian revelation takes the central mystery of human life—creative, suffering, redeeming love— and makes it the explanation of all other mysteries.

"The question which is always being brought forward—'To where, to what, must we educate?'—misunderstands the situation. Only times which know a figure of general validity—the Christian, the gentleman, the citizen—know an answer to that question, not necessarily in words, but by pointing with the finger to the figure which rises clear in the air, out-topping all. The forming of this figure in all individuals, out of all materials, is the formation of a 'culture.' But when all figures are shattered, when no figure is able any more to dominate and shape the present human material, what is there left to form?

"Nothing but the image of God.

"When all 'directions' fail there arises in the darkness over the abyss the one true direction of man, towards the creative Spirit, towards the Spirit of God brooding on the face of the waters, towards Him of whom we know not whence He comes and whither he goes.

"That is man's true autonomy which no longer betrays, but responds.

"Man, the creature, who forms and transforms the creation,

cannot create. But he, each man, can expose himself and others to the creative Spirit. And he can call upon the Creator to save and perfect His image."*

"I, if I be lifted up, will draw all men unto me."†

* Martin Buber: *Between Man and Man*, pp. 102–3.
† St. John xii. 32.

Conclusion of Part II

In this book I have tried to show that the supreme concern of education is with persons, and that the fulfilment of life at the personal level means freedom and community. These values are in greater danger to-day than ever before. The threat to our central value is the great challenge to education to-day. The chief need of our times is for a re-discovery of the value of persons amidst the depersonalizing influences of the modern world.

I have also tried to show (in Part II) that our traditional belief in the sacredness of human personality, which derives historically almost entirely from Christian thought and experience, finds its most uncompromising justification in the Christian doctrine of the loving fatherhood of God. It is no accident that an age which has lost the meaning of Christianity is an age in which personal values are in extreme danger. I have quoted Berdyaev more than once and make no apology for quoting him once more. "The world has entered a period of the agony of the free spirit. Man is shaken to his very foundations by this process of de-humanization. The ideal of man has been eclipsed. This is a trying period, but one of transition. It may be that man must be crucified and die, that he may rise again to new life. Neither Communism nor Fascism is that new life: they are only passing forms in which elements of truth are mingled with frightful untruth and injustice."

How can we in our generation recover our lost religious insight—our lost sense of the reality and presence of God? The Middle Ages were in many ways deplorable—ignorant, violent, and insanitary. But although the people of the Middle Ages may have been much wickeder than we are they never doubted the dependence of this world upon the eternal and the unseen.

The rediscovery of our need of God is obviously the key to the problem. Dr. A. J. Toynbee, speaking of "the attitude of man which sterilized fanaticism at the cost of extinguishing faith," asks: "Will modern Western man repent of and recoil from his ὕβρις before it finds its nemesis in ἄτη?" But it is one thing to hear the call to repentance and another to respond to it.

Perhaps the best way to waken in modern folks a sense of the meaning of religion is not to start with a discussion of God (Who for too many people suggests an old man with a beard, the image of Whom immediately arouses sales resistance), but to help them to realize the religious nature of normal experience —the relation between love, creation, and freedom, and above all the meaning of redemptive love in personal relations, so that they can see that this is indeed the shape and pattern of the world —that life is like that. Then, when they see the Cross uplifted, they will recognize the true meaning of life.

Index